CLASSIFYING PALMPRINTS

Classifying
Palmprints
A Complete System of Coding,
Filing and Searching Palmprints

By

HAROLD L. V. ALEXANDER

Detective Sergeant

Liverpool and Bootle Constabulary

England

CHARLES C THOMAS · PUBLISHER
Springfield · Illinois · U.S.A.

Published and Distributed Throughout the World by

CHARLES C THOMAS • PUBLISHER
Bannerstone House
301-327 East Lawrence Avenue, Springfield, Illinois, U.S.A.

© *1973, by* CHARLES C THOMAS • PUBLISHER
ISBN 0-398-02652-1
Library of Congress Catalog Card Number: 72-86993

With **THOMAS BOOKS** *careful attention is given to all details of
manufacturing and design. It is the Publisher's desire to present books
that are satisfactory as to their physical qualities and artistic possibilities
and appropriate for their particular use.* **THOMAS BOOKS** *will be true
to those laws of quality that assure a good name and good will.*

Printed in the United States of America
HH-11

PREFACE

Since the early days of crime detection, scientists have realized that finger-prints are a positive means of identification. Much has been said and written about fingerprints and fingerprint classifications by many eminent anato-mists and anthropologists. From the works of three such persons, Sir Edward Herschel, Sir Francis Galton, and Sir Edward Henry have evolved our present fingerprint classifications.

Of palmprints and palmprint classifications, very little has been said or written; this must be considered a serious omission in these days of ad-vanced scientific detection. Often, when the only latent print discovered at the scene of a crime is that of a palmar impression, the only means of identifying the owner is by a suggested name.

The palmar classification system was introduced to the Fingerprint De-partment of the Merseyside Criminal Record Office at Liverpool, England, in 1965, mainly because of the lack of palmprint identifications. In the ensuing five years, there was a substantial increase in the number of latent palmprints submitted to the bureau for examination and over 250 of these prints were identified. These facts furnish indisputable evidence that the presence of an efficient palmprint system is a necessary and an integral part of the modern-day bureau.

Classifying Palmprints is one of the first references published on the subject. It has been written, primarily, for the students and members of the public interested in the field of dactylography, that they may more easily understand the intricacy of papillary classification. This manual contains many of the facts collated during the period of study and research which greatly assisted in the compilation of the system. Aspects of coding, taking, searching, and filing, as well as a unique method of coding deltas and loop core formations are graphically discussed. Various tables such as the dis-position of pattern types on the palmar surface, delta types and loop core ridge variations, and a chart indicating the mode, pattern type, and palmar section of identifications are included to assist in the forming of filing systems. The palmprint classification system and statistics will no doubt be of valuable assistance to the experts universally engaged in dactylography, dermatoglyphic research, laboratories, hospitals, and universities research-ing into the relationship between serious illness and the areas of the human body bearing papillary ridges.

Harold L. V. Alexander

v

INTRODUCTION

Prior to the introduction of the classified system and in common with many other fingerprint bureaus, the Merseyside Criminal Record Office at Liverpool had many thousands of palmprints on official forms which were filed in numerical order only.

Consequently, the searching of palmprints found at scences of crime was an almost impossible task, and the scenes of crime collections contained many palmprints which remained undetected.

In order to make better use of palmprints found at the scene of crime, I devised this system of classifying, filing, and searching a palmprint collection which is essentially simple in operation. The time taken to classify a palmprint form is variable, but is $2\frac{1}{2}$ minutes at the maximum. Furthermore, the growth of the palm will not alter the classification.

It is true to say that a palmprint nearly always contains sufficient detail to be used in court proceedings, whereas this cannot be said in respect of fingerprints, owing to the fact that a palmprint clearly contains the greater area of scrutiny. The average palmprint contains some 14 square inches of papillary minutiae, and the ridges traverse the surface in many directions, creating patterns and deltas. The disposition of the various pattern types determines the classification.

It is important to note that it is not necessary for a complete palmprint to have been found at a scene of crime in order that a search of this system be carried out. The classification is so devised that a scene-of-crime mark containing a pattern can be quickly searched in its respective area of the palm, viz. hypothenar, thenar, or triradiate.

The system is divided into four parts:

1. *Primary*. Patterns disclosed in any of the three sections are given a numerical value. This has the effect of segregating the sections—those with patterns and those without.
2. *Secondary*. Describes those patterns disclosed in the hypothenar section.
3. *Tertiary*. Describes those patterns disclosed in the thenar section.
4. *Quaternary*. Describes those patterns disclosed in the triradiate section according to their disposition.

Preference has been given to the section most frequently found at a scene of crime, namely the hypothenar, but by the elimination of certain of the primary

vii

classifications, it becomes a simple matter to search a pattern which occurs in the thenar or triradiate sections.

Three subclassifications are used to speed the search of the more congested parts of the classifications:

1. Two sets of ridge count when a single loop or tented arch formation is disclosed in the triradiate section.
2. A delta classification when the hypothenar section is devoid of pattern— about 62 percent of palmprints recorded.
3. A core classification based on the number of ridge characteristics within the core of a single loop formation disclosed in the hypothenar section— about 20 percent of palmprints recorded.

Subclassifications 2 and 3 were incorporated into the system in 1968. It is worthy of note, to those persons interested in dermatological research, that each classification bears its own main line of configuration. Palmprints filed in classification order will group together the many varied lines of configuration, making it a simple matter to retrieve any line of configuration under review.

H. L. V. A.

ACKNOWLEDGMENTS

The author wishes to thank all those persons who kindly volunteered their knowledge, advice, and above all their palmprints.

A special acknowledgment is extended to the staff of the Fingerprint and Photographic Department of the Merseyside Criminal Record Office in Liverpool, England, whose most valuable assistance made the production of this book possible.

H. L. V. A.

CONTENTS

CLASSIFYING PALMPRINTS

Chapter I

BASIS FOR CODING

For the purposes of the classification, the palmar area is divided into three sections as shown in Figure 1.

Hypothenar. Area beneath the triradiate section on the little finger side. It is bounded by the distal transverse crease on the top and the radial longitudinal crease on the side.

Thenar. Area beneath the triradiate section on the thumb side. It is completely enclosed by the radial longitudinal crease.

Triradiate. Otherwise known as the interdigital area, is situated beneath the base of the fingers and is enclosed by the metacarpo phalangeal creases and the distal transverse crease.

To provide a base for coding this system of classification, the flow of ridges as disclosed in Figure 2 is considered to be *normal* in that no pattern is disclosed. The inverted arch formation at the base of the ring finger in the triradiate section is not considered to be a pattern.

Normal Flow

1. In the hypothenar section the ridges tend to flow in a near horizontal manner at the base and then in an upward slant which approaches the perpendicular when the ridges merge with the thenar section.

2. In the thenar section the ridges tend to flow in a near perpendicular curve, similar to a large arch formation.

3. In the triradiate section the ridges tend to traverse the palm in a near horizontal manner except at the deltas where the three ridge streams meet.

Any deviation from the flow depicted in Figure 2 will be recorded as a pattern according to the definitions.

DEMARCATION OF PALMAR SURFACE

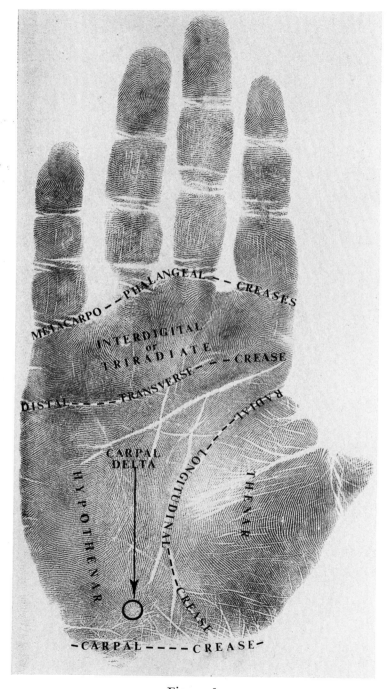

Figure 1.

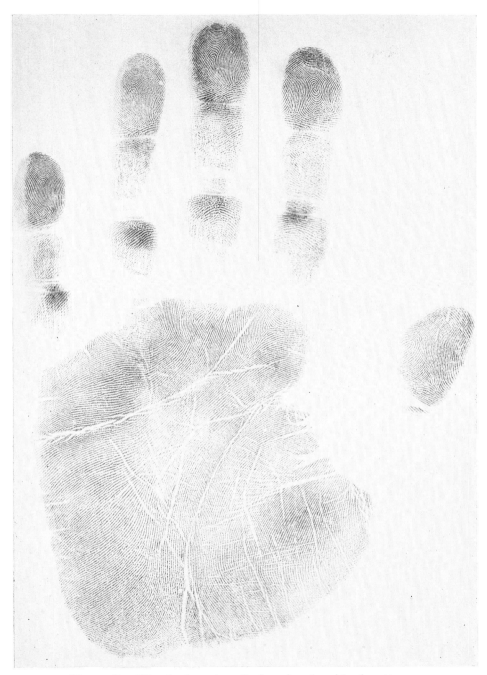

Figure 2. The basic palm. Left palm devoid of patterns.

DIAGRAM I

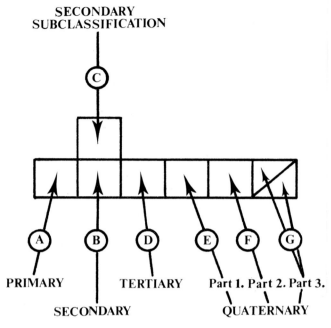

RECOMMENDED CODING BOX

It is of utmost importance that the details of each sectional classification are recorded in the correct square of the coding box.

The squares of the coding box are lettered for reference purposes and to assist in the association of the various sectional classifications with the appropriate square.

Primary Classification. Square "A"

Numerically indicates the presence or absence of patterns in the hypothenar, thenar, and triradiate sections.

Secondary Classification. Square "B"

Symbol(s) indicate the type of pattern(s) or delta disclosed in the hypo thenar section.

Subsecondary Classification. Square "C"

A symbol or numeral indicates, in certain cases, the loop or delta classification disclosed in the hypothenar section.

Tertiary Classification. Square "D"

Symbol(s) indicate pattern(s) disclosed in the thenar section.

Quaternary Classification. Part 1. Square "E"

Symbol(s) indicate pattern(s) disclosed in the triradiate section.

Quaternary Classification. Part 2. Square "F"

Numerically indicates the disposition of pattern(s) disclosed in the triradiate section.

Quaternary Classification. Part 3. Square "G"

Ridge counts of certain single patterns disclosed in the triradiate section.

Chapter II

PRIMARY CLASSIFICATION

The primary classification numerically indicates the sectional disposition of patterns disclosed on the palmar surface.

The presence of a pattern in any of the three sections is signified by the numeric values set out in Table I, the sum of which is recorded in square "A" of the coding box.

If the palm is devoid of pattern in *all three* sections, the primary classification is recorded as 1.

If more than one pattern is disclosed in any *one* section, the same numeric value applies as if only one pattern is present.

If patterns are disclosed in more than one section, the appropriate values are added together, thus recording the primary classification for the palm as a whole.

TABLE I

PRIMARY VALUES

Pattern	Symbol	Thenar	Triradiate	Hypothenar
Whorl A core	A	2	3	4
Whorl B core	B	2	3	4
Twined loop	T.L.	2	3	4
Lateral pocket loop	L.P.	2	3	4
Central pocket loop	C.P.	2	3	4
Accidentals and composites	A.C.C.	2	3	4
Tented arch	T	2	3	4
Loop core *inward*	I	2	3	4
Loop core *outward*	0	2	3	4
Loop core *downward*	D	2	3	4
Loop core *upward*	U	2	3	4
Loop core *nutant*	K	2	3	4
Nondescript	N	2	3	4
Plain arch	N	—	—	4

EXAMPLES OF THE PRIMARY CLASSIFICATION

Primary Value 1. This denotes a complete absence of pattern in any section (Fig. 3).

Primary Value 2. Any pattern(s) in the thenar section—*none* in any other (Fig. 4).

Primary Value 3. Any pattern(s) in the triradiate section—*none* in any other (Fig. 5).

Primary Value 4. Any pattern(s) in the hypothenar section—*none* in any other (Fig. 6).

Primary Value 5. A combination of any pattern(s) in both the thenar and triradiate—*none* in the hypothenar section (Fig. 7).

Primary Value 6. A combination of pattern(s) in both thenar and hypothenar sections—*none* in the triradiate section (Fig. 8.)

Primary Value 7. A combination of pattern(s) in both the triradiate and hypothenar—*none* in the thenar section (Fig. 9).

Primary Value 9. A combination of pattern(s) in all three sections (Fig. 10).

(The primary value of classification 8 is unobtainable.)

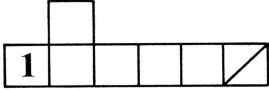

Figure 3. Left palm.

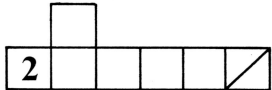

Figure 4.   Left palm.

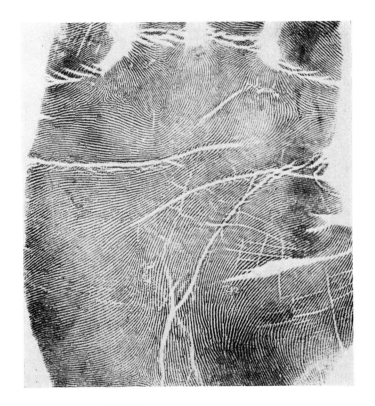

Figure 5. Left palm.

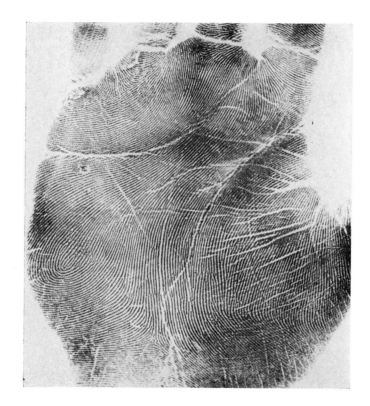

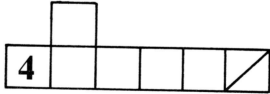

Figure 6. Left palm.

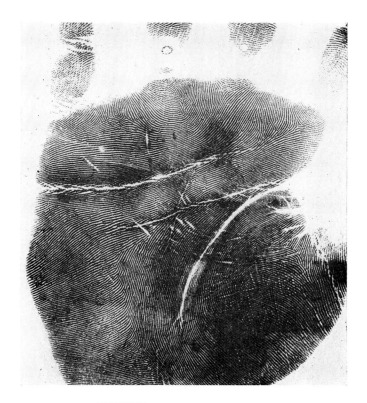

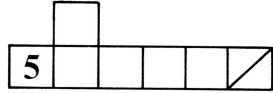

Figure 7. Left palm.

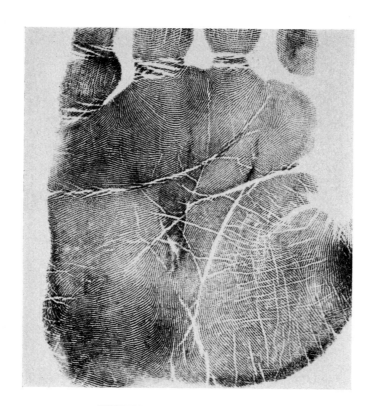

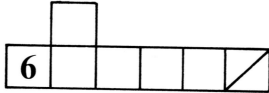

Figure 8. Left palm.

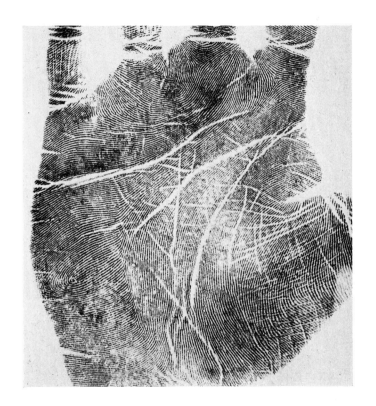

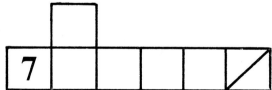

Figure 9.   Left palm.

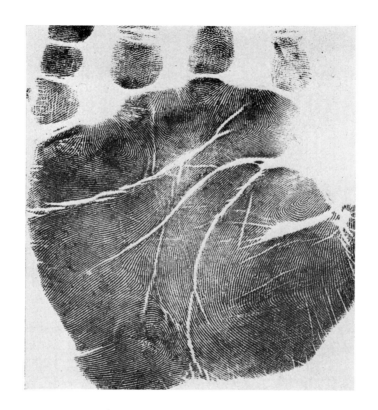

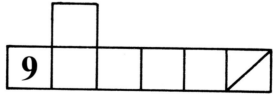

Figure 10. Left Palm.

Chapter III

SECONDARY AND SECONDARY SUBCLASSIFICATION

For the purposes of the secondary classification the hypothenar section *only* is used.

The symbol denoting the type of pattern disclosed in this section is recorded in square "B" of the coding box (Fig. 11).

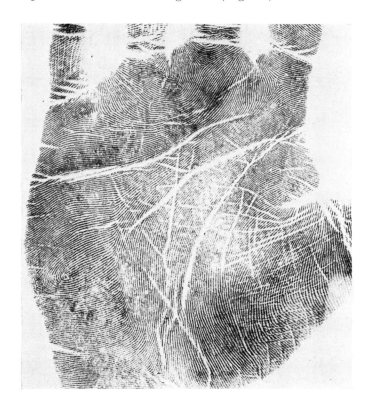

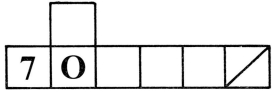

Figure 11. Left palm.

If more than one pattern is disclosed in the hypothenar section, the pattern closest to the triradiate section is recorded first above any other symbol (Fig. 12).

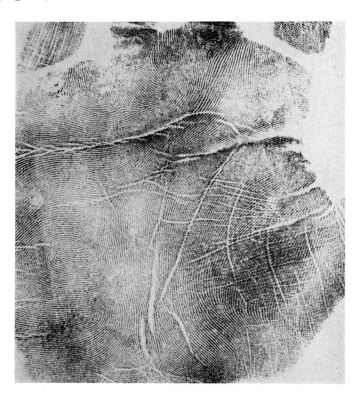

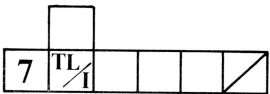

Figure 12.   Left palm.

If the hypothenar section is devoid of pattern, the position of the carpal delta is recorded and the following symbols are used: "H" for high delta (Fig. 13); "L" for low delta in normal position (Fig. 14).

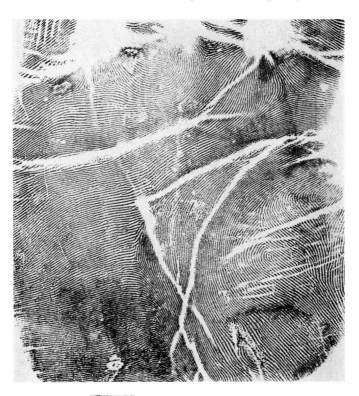

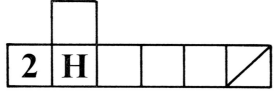

Figure 13.　Left palm.

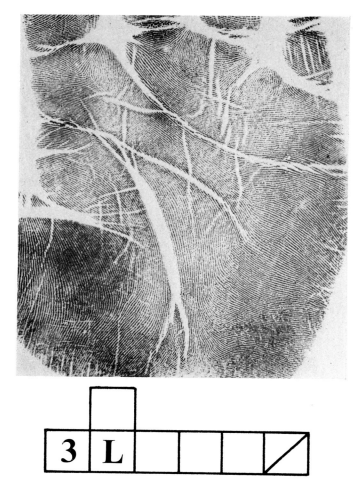

Figure 14.   Right palm.

If the carpal delta is not shown on the palmprint form due to (a) bad taking or (b) none disclosed, the symbol "L" is used.

Secondary Subclassification

1. In *all* cases where a *single* loop formation is present in the hypothenar section, the number of ridge characteristics within the core area is recorded in square "C" of the coding box (see definitions).

2. In *all* cases where the hypothenar section is devoid of pattern and the position of the carpal delta is recorded, the delta classification is recorded in square "C" of the coding box (see definitions).

Chapter IV

TERTIARY CLASSIFICATION

The symbol denoting any pattern disclosed in the thenar section is recorded in square "D" of the coding box (Figs. 15 and 16).

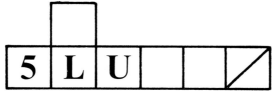

Figure 15.   Right palm.

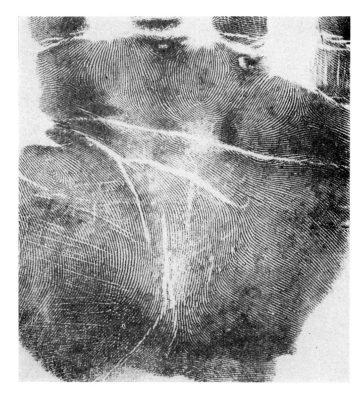

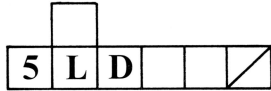

Figure 16.   Right palm.

If more than one pattern is disclosed in the thenar section, the pattern closest to the triradiate section is recorded first above any other symbol (Figs. 17 and 18).

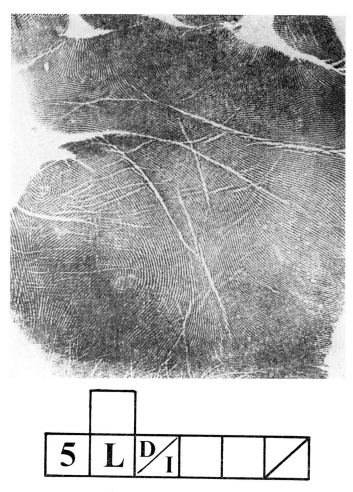

Figure 17. Right palm.

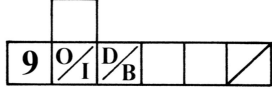

Figure 18. Left palm.

Chapter V

QUATERNARY CLASSIFICATION

PART 1, 2, and 3

PART 1. PATTERN TYPE

The symbol denoting any pattern disclosed in the triradiate section is recorded in square "E" of the coding box (Figs. 19 and 20).

If more than one pattern is disclosed, the pattern closest to the forefinger is recorded first and above any other symbol (Figs. 21, 22, 23, and 24).

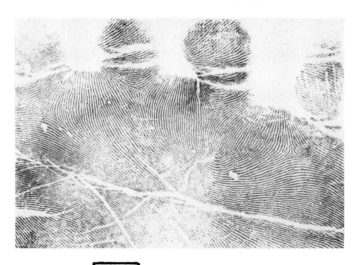

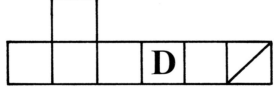

Figure 19.   Right palm.

188

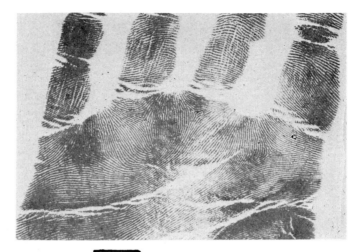

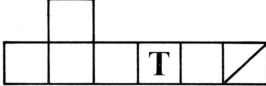

Figure 20.   Left palm.

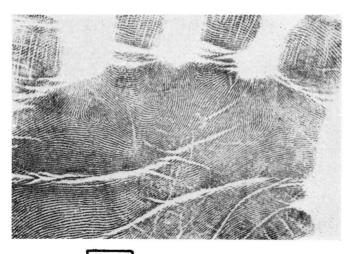

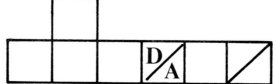

Figure 21.   Left palm.

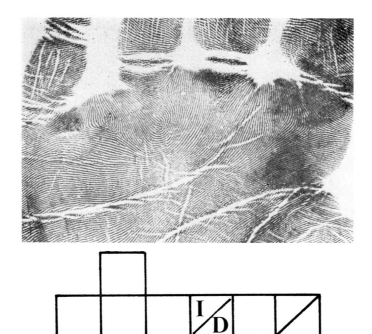

Figure 22.   Left palm.

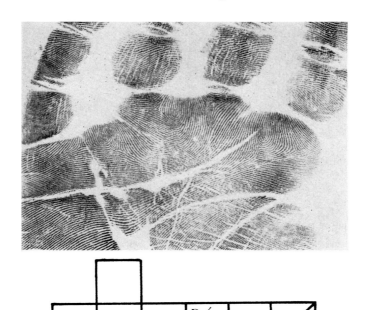

Figure 23.   Left palm.

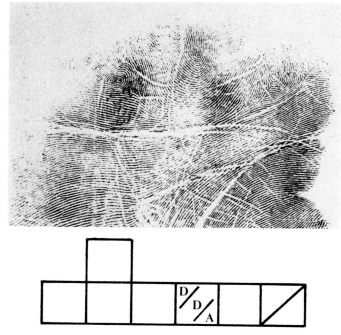

Figure 24.   Left palm.

PART 2.   NUMERICAL VALUE

The position of any pattern disclosed in Part 1 is denoted by a numerical value according to the position in relation to the base of the fingers (Fig. 25) and is recorded in square "F" of the coding box (Figs. 26, 27, and 28).

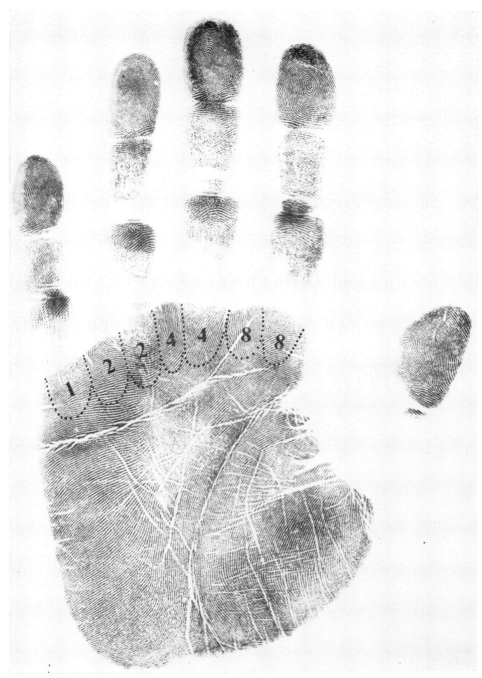

Figure 25. Left palm, showing numeric value of patterns in triradiate.

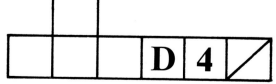

Figure 26.   Right palm.

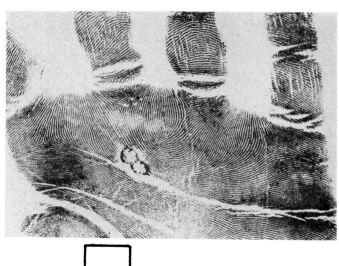

Figure 27.   Right palm.

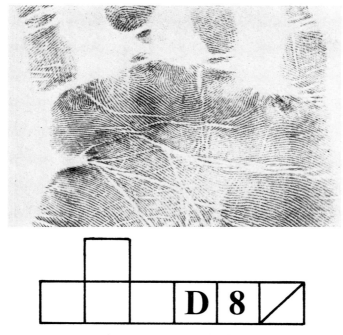

Figure 28.   Right palm.

Pattern originating under the forefinger—value 8.

Pattern originating under the middle finger—value 4.

Pattern originating under the ring finger—value 2.

Pattern originating under the little finger—value 1.

When a pattern originates between two fingers it is assumed to originate under the finger with the higher value, e.g. between the middle and ring fingers the value would be 4 (Figs. 25 and 27).

If more than one pattern is disclosed, the sum of each is recorded (Figs. 29, 30, 31, 32, 33, and 34).

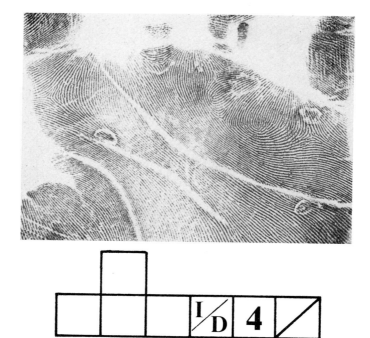

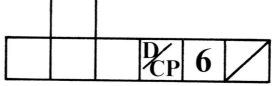

Figure 29.   Right palm.

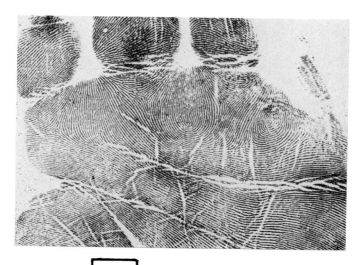

Figure 30.   Right palm.

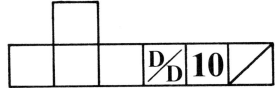

Figure 31. Right palm.

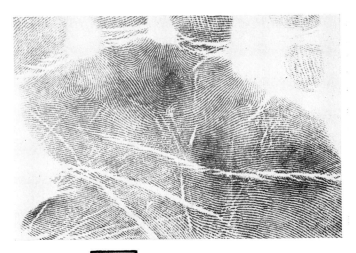

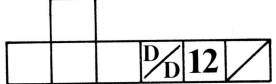

Figure 32. Right palm.

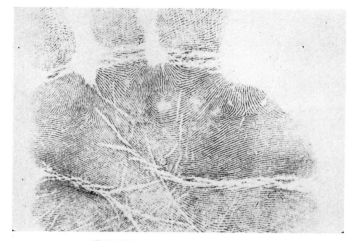

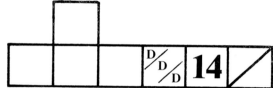

Figure 33.   Right palm.

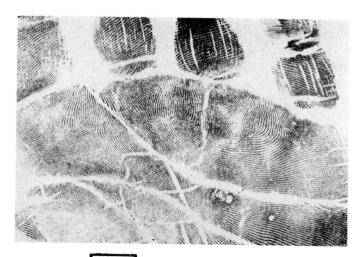

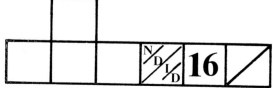

Figure 34.   Right palm.

PART 3. RIDGE COUNT

In this section of the palm, the incidence rate of some pattern types is far greater than in others. This causes overcrowding in certain classifications and difficulty is experienced when searching a latent print, or retrieving from the collection a form bearing one of these pattern types. To obviate this, when *one* of these patterns is disclosed a ridge count is used.

Where only one of the following pattern types is disclosed, a ridge count is recorded in square "G" of the coding box.

"T"—tented arch.

"I"—loop core inward.

O"—loop core outward. This pattern is rarely disclosed in this section but has been included for filing purposes.

"D"—loop core downward.

Where any other pattern, or *two or more patterns* of any type are disclosed, a ridge count is *not* recorded.

On the Right Hand

In all cases, the ridge count from the core of the pattern to the nearest delta on the *right* is recorded on the bottom and the ridge count from the core of the pattern to the nearest delta on the *left* is recorded above (Fig. 35).

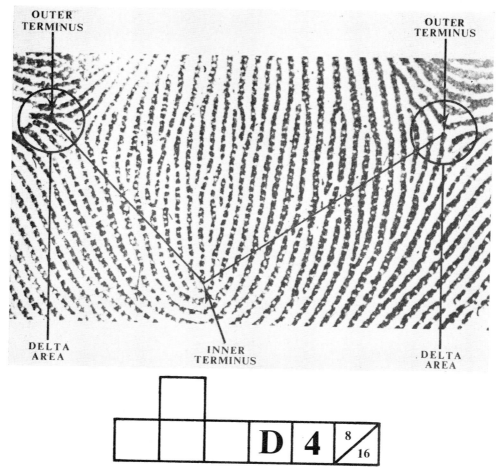

Figure 35. Downward "D" loop formation on right palm. Ridge counts.

On the Left Hand

In all cases, the ridge count from the core of the pattern to the nearest delta on the *left* is recorded on the bottom and the ridge count from the core of the pattern to the nearest delta on the *right* is recorded above (Figs. 36 and 37).

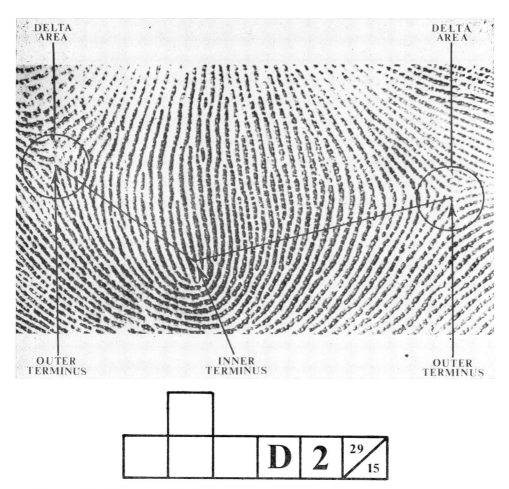

Figure 36. Downward "D" loop formation on left palm. Ridge counts.

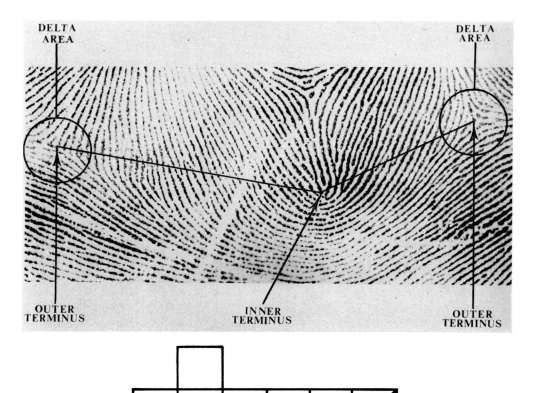

Figure 37.   Tented arch "T" formation on left palm.   Ridge counts.

Chapter VI

DEFINITIONS
FIXED POINTS — OUTER AND INNER TERMINI — RIDGE COUNTS

FIXED POINTS

F*or use in the Triradiate Section Only*

In the tented arch and loop patterns, there are fixed points in determining the ridge count:

1. The delta area and outer terminus (Figs. 38, 39, 40, 41, and 42).

2. The core or inner terminus (Figs. 43, 44, 45, 46, 47, and 48).

The use of fixed points for the ridge count is *only* required in the quaternary classification—*Part 3* when a single tented arch or loop formation is present.

FIXED POINTS—OUTER TERMINUS

Delta Area and Outer Terminus

1. Where the delta is formed by a bifurcation, the point or bifurcation is the outer terminus (Figs. 38 and 39).

2. Where there are several such bifurcations, the one nearest to the core is the outer terminus (Fig. 40).

3. Where the delta is formed by the abrupt divergence of two ridges which have hitherto run side by side, the nearest ridge in front of the place where the divergence begins, even if it be a mere point and whether it is independent of, or sprung from the diverging ridge or not, is the outer terminus (Figs. 41 and 42).

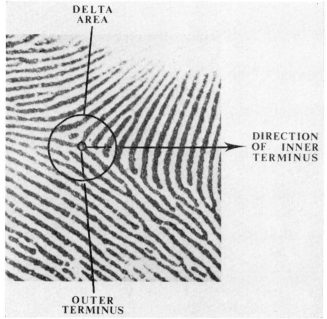

Figure 38.   Delta formation. This delta is formed by a ridge which bifurcates; the precise position of the outer terminus is indicated.

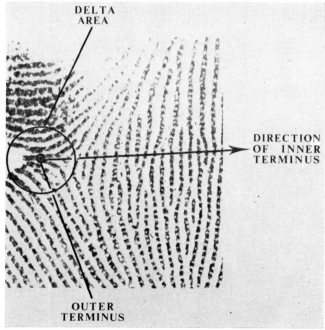

Figure 39.   Delta formation. This delta is formed by a ridge which bifurcates; the precise position of the outer terminus is indicated.

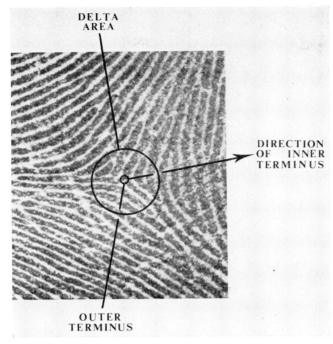

Figure 40. Delta formation. This delta is formed by a ridge bearing several bifurcations; the precise position of the outer terminus is indicated.

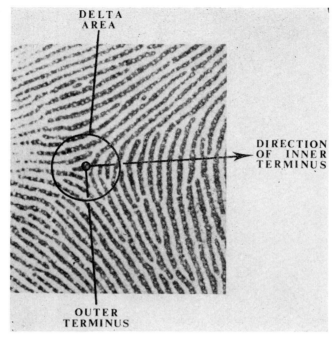

Figure 41.   Delta formation. This delta is formed by diverging ridges which have hitherto run side by side; the precise position of the outer terminus in indicated.

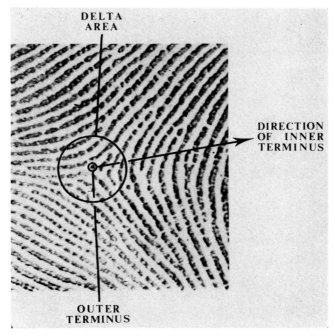

Figure 42. Delta formation. This delta is formed by diverging ridges which have hitherto run side by side; the precise position of the outer terminus is indicated.

FIXED POINTS—INNER TERMINUS

Tented Arch and Loop — Core or Inner Terminus

Departure from the Henry system of defining the core or inner terminus is necessary due to the presence of two sets of ridge counts. *In both patterns:*

1. The rod nearest to the recurving staple is the core or inner terminus (Figs. 43, 44, 45, and 46).

2. In the absence of a central rod(s), the top of the recurving staple is the core or inner terminus (Fig. 47).

3. In the case of two rods of equal length, it is assumed the two rods recurve (Fig. 48).

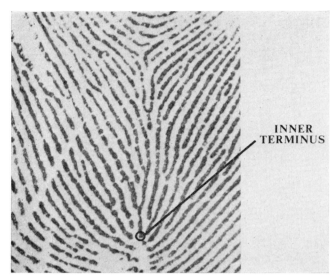

Figure 43.   Tented arch formation. In this case, two or more rods of unequal length are enclosed by the recurving ridge; the precise position of the inner terminus is indicated.

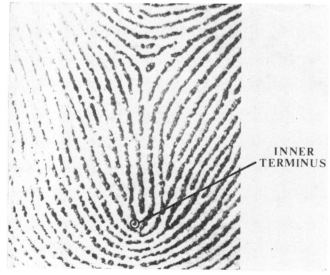

Figure 44.   Tented arch formation. In this case, two or more rods of unequal length are enclosed by the recurving ridge; the precise position of the inner terminus is indicated.

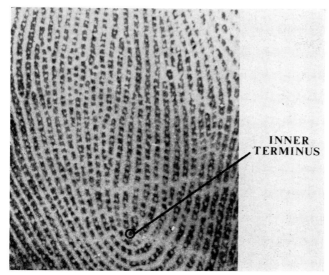

Figure 45. Loop formation. In this case, two or more rods of unequal length are enclosed by the recurving ridge; the precise position of the inner terminus is indicated.

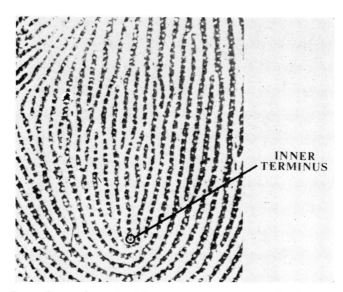

Figure 46. Loop formation. In this case, two or more rods of unequal length are enclosed by the recurving ridge; the precise position of the inner terminus is indicated.

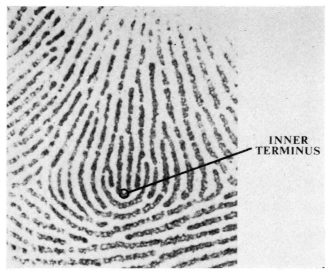

Figure 47. Loop formation. In this case, there is an absence of rod(s) within the recurving ridge; the precise position of the inner terminus is indicated.

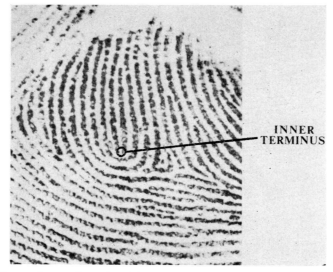

Figure 48. Loop formation. In this case, two rods of equal length are enclosed by the recurving ridge; the precise position of the inner terminus is indicated.

RIDGE COUNTS

The number of ridges cut by an imaginary line drawn from the *outer terminus* to the *core* or *inner terminus* are counted, excluding *both* ridges that form the *outer and inner termini* (Figs. 35, 36, and 37).

Chapter VII

PATTERN DEFINITIONS

Whorl "A" Various Types

1. The ridges make a turn through *one* complete circuit.

2. The ridges consist of concentric circles.

3. The ridges in the centre commence with a single spiral.

4. The ridges in the centre commence with a double spiral.

All cores are small and circular (Figs. 49, 50, 51, and 52).

Figure 49.   Right palm.   Pattern in hypothenar.

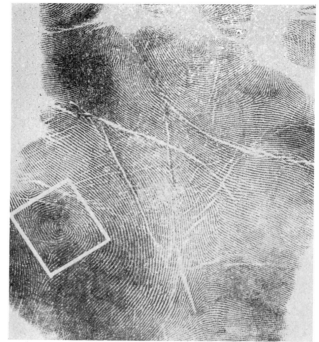

Figure 50.   Right palm.   Pattern in thenar.

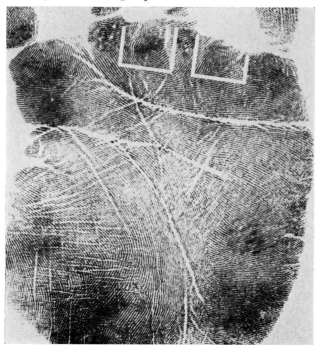

Figure 51.   Right palm.   Patterns in triradiate.

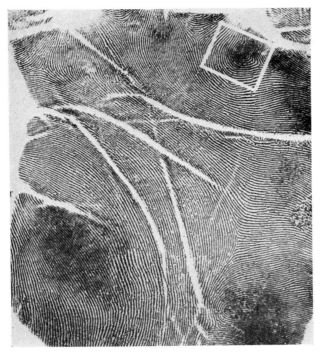

Figure 52. Right palm. Pattern in triradiate.

Whorl "B"

The ridges in the centre are elliptical or almond shape (Figs. 53, 54, and 55).

This pattern is rarely recorded in the triradiate section.

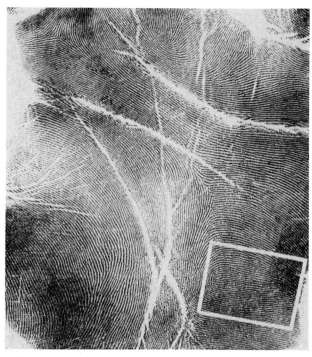

Figure 53. Right palm. Pattern in hypothenar.

Figure 54. Right palm. Pattern in hypothenar.

Figure 55. Left palm. Pattern in thenar.

Twined Loop "TL"

The ridges consist of two well-defined loops, one superincumbent on or surrounding the other. The deltas are on the *outside* of the loops (Figs. 56, 57, 58, and 59).

This pattern is rarely recorded in the triradiate section.

Where a delta divides the two loops it is *not* recorded as a twined loop but two separate patterns depending on the slope and flow of the patterns, e.g. outer "O" and inner "I" loops (Fig. 60).

The same will apply if this occurs in either the thenar or triradiate sections.

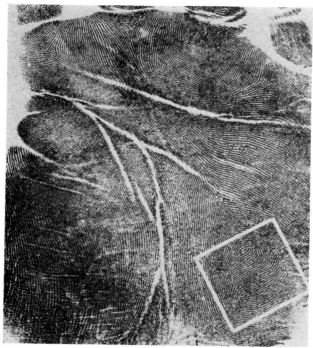

Figure 56.   Right palm. Pattern in hypothenar.

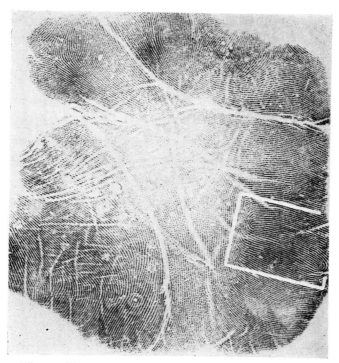

Figure 57. Right palm. Pattern in hypothenar.

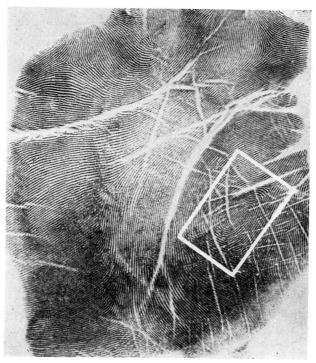

Figure 58. Left palm. Pattern in thenar.

Figure 59. Right palm. Pattern in thenar.

Figure 60. Left palm. Pattern in hypothenar.

Lateral Pocket Loop "LP"

When the ridges constituting the loop bend sharply on one side before recurving, thereby forming on that side an interspace or pocket ordinarily filled with ridges of another loop. Attention is drawn to the fact that in this pattern the cores of the two loops are more or less at right angles to one another (Figs. 61, 62, 63, 64, and 65).

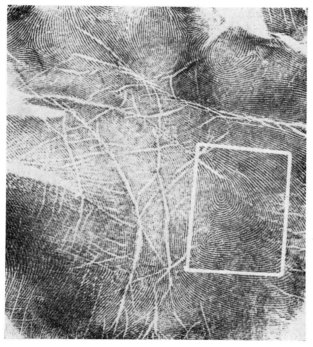

Figure 61. Right palm. Pattern in hypothenar.

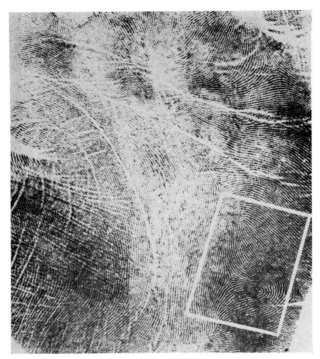

Figure 62. Right palm. Pattern in hypothenar.

Figure 63. Left palm. Pattern in thenar.

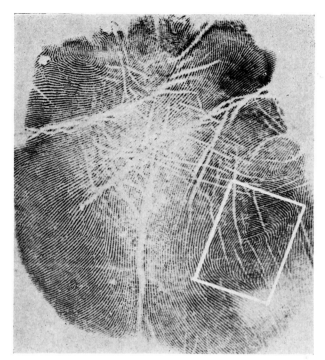

Figure 64.   Left palm.   Pattern in thenar.

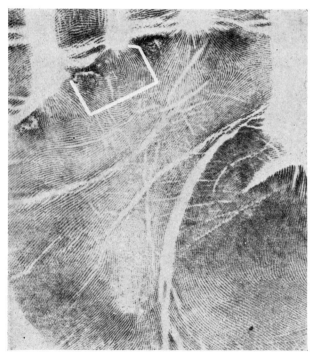

Figure 65.   Left palm.   Pattern in triradiate.

Central Pocket Loop "CP"

In some patterns of the loop type, the ridges about the core deviate in course from the general course of other ridges and by turning back will form a convergence in the core. The converging ridges form a kind of pocket and give rise to the appearance of a second delta formation (Figs. 66, 67, 68, 69, 70, and 71).

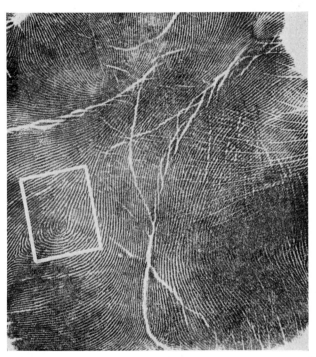

Figure 66.   Left palm.   Pattern in hypothenar.

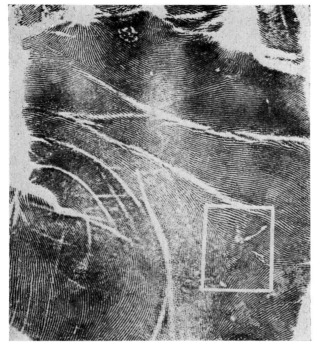

Figure 67.   Right palm.   Pattern in hypothenar.

Figure 68.   Left palm.   Pattern in thenar.

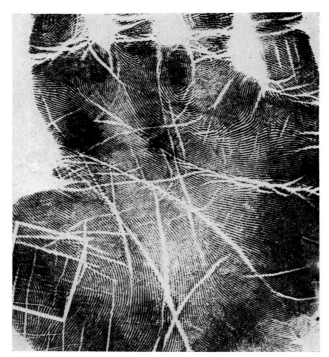

Figure 69. Right palm. Pattern in thenar.

Figure 70. Left palm. Pattern in triradiate.

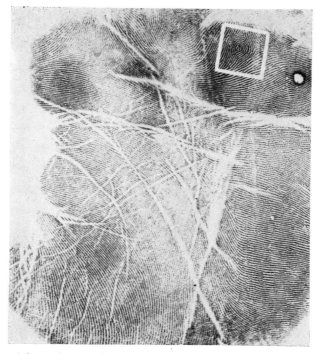

Figure 71.   Right palm.   Pattern in triradiate.

Accidental and Composite "A.C.C."

Patterns whose formation do not conform to the arch, loop or whorl type yet possess characteristics common to all three *or* pattern comprising two or more patterns (Figs. 72 and 73).

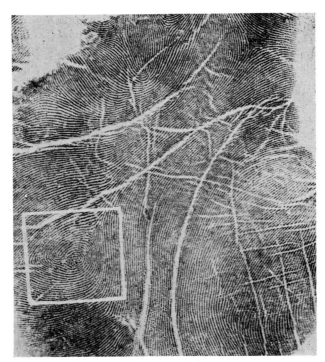

Figure 72.   Left palm.   Pattern in hypothenar.

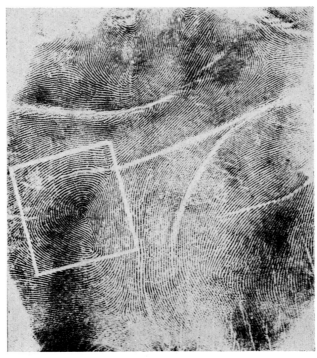

Figure 73.   Left palm.   Pattern in hypothenar.

Tented Arch "T"

In some patterns of the arch type, the ridges near the middle have a definite thrust away from the platform ridge, arranging themselves on both sides of a central axis or central spine towards which adjoining ridges converge. The pattern appears as a tent in outline (Figs. 74 and 75).

Demarcating the line which separates tented arches and loops whose ridges have a vertical trend, it is held that if on either side of the axis one ridge recurves, the impression is a loop provided a ridge count can be obtained. If, however, a ridge recurves on both sides of the vertical ridge or axis, then the impression should be regarded as two loops.

Figure 74.   Right palm.   Pattern in triradiate.

Figure 75.   Right palm.   Pattern in both triradiate and hypothenar.

Loop Formations

The ridges in the core make a backward turn but without a twist.

Inward Loop "I"

Where the core of the loop is innermost and the flow of ridges is from the outside edge of the palm.

In the hypothenar section, the core of the loop points towards the thenar section (Fig. 76). In this section *only* the single loop formation is further subclassified (see definitions) and recorded in square "C" of the coding box.

In the thenar section, the core of the loop points towards the hypothenar section (Fig. 77). (Note the direction of slope of the inner loop "I" which is at right angles to the downward loop "D" in this section (Fig. 79); also compare the direction of slope between the inner loop "I" in Figure 79 and the upper loop "U" in Figure 86).

In the triradiate section, the core of the loop and the general flow of ridges slope markedly toward the thenar section (Fig. 78). Only those loop formations with a projected direction of slope within the perimeters of (1) the extreme outside edge of the metacarpo phalangeal crease of the forefinger, and (2) the extreme outside and top edge of the thumb and thenar crease should be recorded as an inner loop "I" formation.

Any loop formation whose projected direction of slope is beneath that of the item 2 perimeter should be recorded as a downward loop "D" formation.

Figure 76.   Right palm.   Pattern in hypothenar.

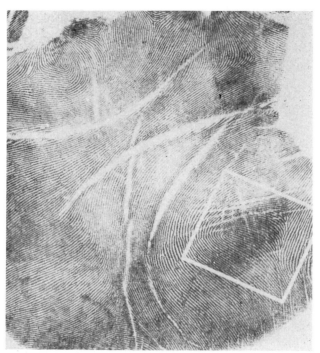

Figure 77.   Left palm.   Pattern in thenar.

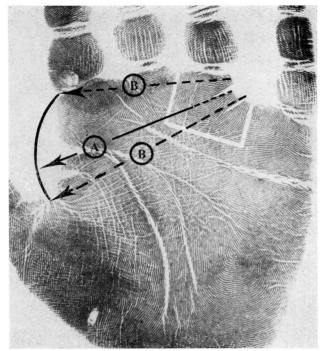

Figure 78. Right palm. Pattern in triradiate. (A), Direction of slope of loop formation; (B), limitations within which the projected direction of slope must fall.

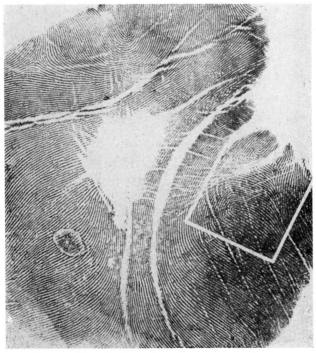

Figure 79. Left palm. Pattern in thenar.

Outward Loop "O"

Where the core of the loop points towards the outside edge and the flow of ridges is to the inside of the palm (Fig. 80). This type is rarely recorded in the thenar and triradiate sections.

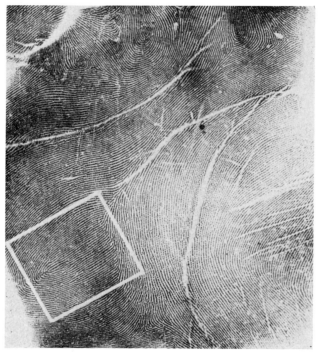

Figure 80.   Left palm.   Pattern in hypothenar.

In the hypothenar the single loop formation is further subclassified (see definitions) and recorded in square "C" of the coding box.

Downward "D"

Where the ridges of the loop originate above the recurve and slope or flow downward in a near perpendicular manner pointing towards the carpal border of the palm (Figs. 81, 82, and 83).

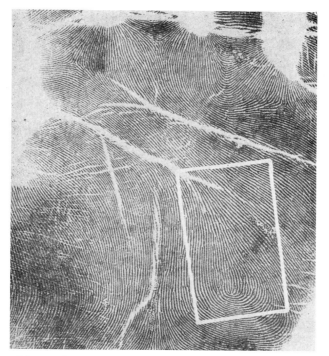

Figure 81.   Right palm.   Pattern in hypothenar.

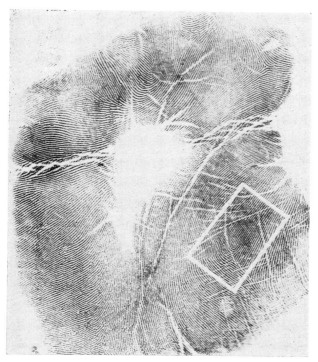

Figure 82.   Left palm.   Pattern in thenar.

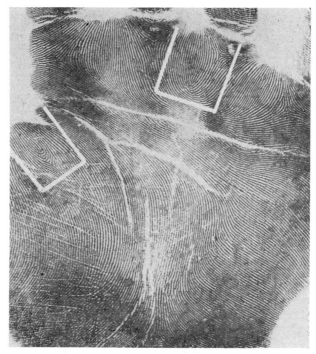

Figure 83.   Left palm.   Pattern in both thenar and triradiate.

In the hypothenar section, the single loop formation is further subclassi-
(see definitions) and recorded in square "C" of the coding box. (Note the
difference between this loop formation and the nutant "K" loop formation
in Figure 87).

Upward "U"

Where the ridges of the loop originate below the recurve and slope or
flow upward in a near perpendicular manner pointing toward the triradiate
section (Figs. 84 and 85).

In the hypothenar section, the single loop formation is further subclassified (see definitions) and recorded in square "C" of the coding box.

This type of loop is rarely recorded in the triradiate section.

Compare the directions of slope between the upper loop "U" in Figure
86 and the inner loop "I" in Figure 79.

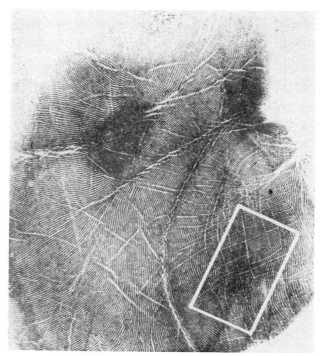

Figure 84.   Left palm.   Pattern in thenar.

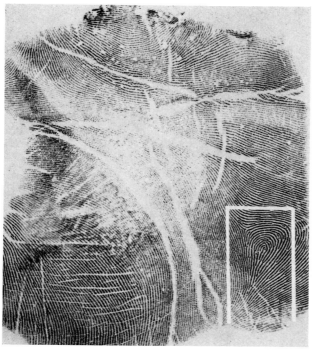

Figure 85.   Right palm.   Pattern in hypothenar.

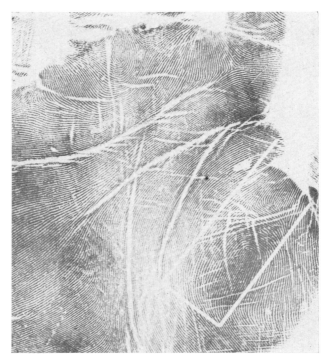

Figure 86.   Left palm.   Pattern in thenar.

Nutant "K"

HYPOTHENAR SECTION. Where the ridges of a downward loop "D" display a sharp bend or deviation towards the carpal delta (Fig. 87).

In this section, the single loop formation is further subclassified (see definitions) and recorded in square "C" of the coding box.

THENAR SECTION. Where the ridges show a sharp bend or deviation (Fig. 88).

This type of loop is rarely recorded in the triradiate section. (Note the difference between downward "D" loop in Figure 81 and nutant "K" loop in Figure 87).

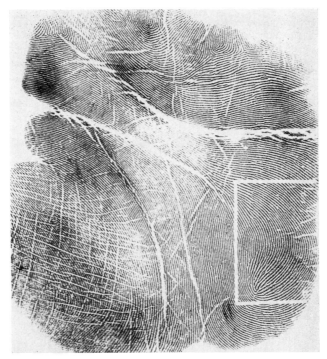

Fibure 87. Right palm. Pattern in hypothenar.

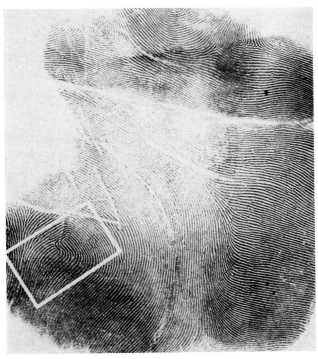

Figure 88. Right palm. Pattern in thenar.

Nondescript "N"

Ridges which *do not* conform to any pattern but where the ridges are almost at right angles to the normal flow—no recurve is present (Figs. 89 and 90).

Figure 89.   Right palm.   Pattern in thenar.

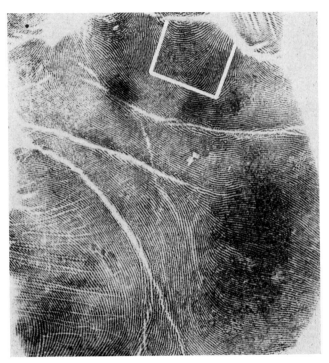

Figure 90.   Right palm.   Pattern in triradiate.

In the hypothenar section *only* a plain arch formation is recorded as a nondescript "N" (Figs. 91 and 92).

Arch

Where the ridges flow from side to side making no backward turn.

HYPOTHENAR SECTION. In this section *only* is the arch formation recorded (Figs. 91 and 92) using the symbol "N" in the classification in square "B" of the coding box.

THENAR SECTION. The arch formation is *not* recorded. Normal flow of ridges in this section appears as a large arch formation (Fig. 2).

TRIRADIATE SECTION. The arch formation is *not* recorded.

Figure 91. Right palm. Pattern in hypothenar.

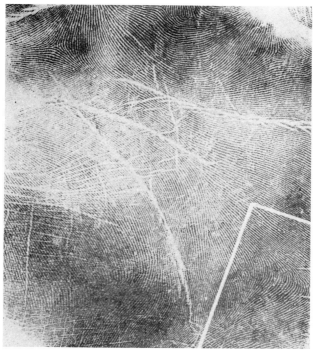

Figure 92. Right palm. Pattern in hypothenar.

Chapter VIII

DEFINITION OF HIGH AND LOW DELTAS

CARPAL DELTA

W hen the hypothenar section is devoid of pattern, the position of the carpal delta is recorded as the secondary classification in square "B" of the coding box.

High Delta "H"

Where the carpal delta is nearer to the triradiate section than is usual and the ridges forming the inner side of the delta flow in a perpendicular manner (Fig. 93).

Figure 93. Right palm. White marker indicates perpendicular flow of ridges on inner side of delta.

78

Low Delta "L"

Where the carpal delta is in a normal position and the ridges forming the base of the delta flow in a horizontal manner (Fig. 94).

Normally, no difficulty is experienced in deciding whether a delta should be classified as "H" or "L." If, however, a doubt exists and the above principle cannot be applied, it should be recorded as "L."

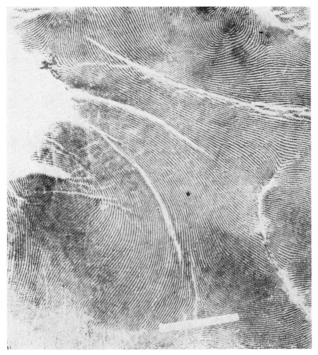

Figure 94. Right palm. White marker indicates horizontal flow of base ridges of delta.

In both cases, the carpal delta is further subclassified (see definitions) and is recorded in square "C" of the coding box.

In cases where *more than one* delta is disclosed and no pattern exists, their relevant positions in the hypothenar section are recorded in square "B" of the coding box. They are recorded in the same manner as any double or multipattern and are filed accordingly. The deltas are *not* subclassified.

Chapter IX

DEFINITIONS
LOOP CORE CLASSIFICATION AND DELTA TYPES

SUBCLASSIFICATION OF SINGLE LOOPS PRESENT IN THE HYPOTHENAR SECTION

Owing to the large number of loops present in the hypothenar section, especially those of the outer "O" type, it has been found necessary to subclassify the following single loop formations present in this section of the palm:

1.	Inner	"I"
2.	Outer	"O"
3.	Downward	"D"
4.	Upward	"U"
5.	Nutant	"K"

A Battley Single Fingerprint Coding Glass (Fig. 95) is only used in this part of the classification; the remainder of the classification requires no special optical apparatus.

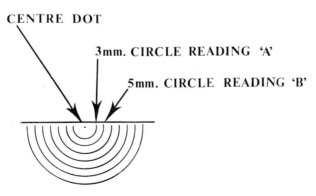

CENTRE DOT

3mm. CIRCLE READING 'A'

5mm. CIRCLE READING 'B'

Figure 95.   Base of coding glass—actual size.

The subclassification is based on the number of ridge characteristics present in the core area within the two following described perimeters (Figs. 96 to 99A):

1. The second recurving ridge of the loop whether partial or complete

providing the recurve extends past the loop apex, and where it is a partial recurve, one leg must extend past the 3mm. circle reading "A" on the glass (Figs. 99 and 99A).

2. The 5mm. circle reading "B" on the glass—to both points where perimeters "A" and "B" bisect (Fig. 96).

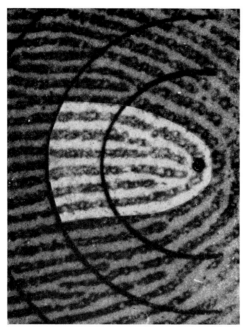

Figure 96.   The area of scrutiny is the lighter section which is surrounded by the darkened perimeter. (Note: The theory is explained in Fig. 97.)

Method

The centre dot of the glass is placed on the apex of the *first* recurving ridge of the loop, and both legs of the loop staple must extend to or beyond the 3mm. circle reading "A" (Figs. 97 to 99A). The number of ridge characteristics present within the two perimeters is recorded in square "C" of the coding box.

All characteristics attached to or enclosed by the *first* recurving ridge are included, but characteristics attached to or *not fully* enclosed by the *second* recurving ridge are excluded (Fig. 97).

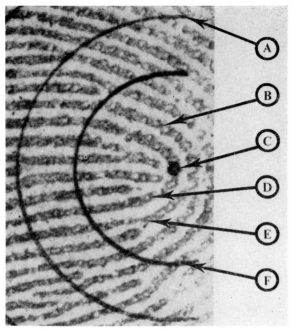

Figure 97.   Loop core disclosing four ridge characteristics. (A), 5mm. circle reading "B" on coding glass and perimeter "B"; (B), second recurving ridge and perimeter "A"; (C), centre dot on coding glass; (D), first recurving ridge; (E), excluded characteristic; (F), 3mm. circle reading "A" on coding glass.

If a delta is present within the 3mm. circle reading "A" on the glass, the classification is recorded as "O" (zero). In some cases, a second recurve does not exist due to the presence of the delta.

A dot, a ridge end, or bifurcation is regarded as one characteristic. An independent ridge, a lake, a spur, or, with one exception, a crossover as two characteristics. The exception arises where the first and second recurving ridges are joined by a crossover. In this case, only the attachment to the first recurving ridge is recorded, i.e. one characteristic.

Figure 98.   Actual size. Coding glass is correctly set in position on core of the loop formation.

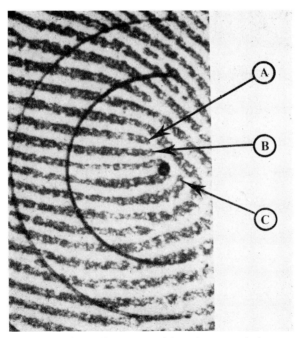

Figure 98A.   Figure 98 enlarged. Three ridge characteristics are disclosed within the specified perimeters and are marked A, B, and C.

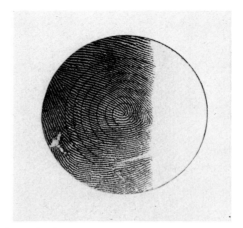

Figure 99. Actual size. Coding glass is correctly set in position on core of the loop formation.

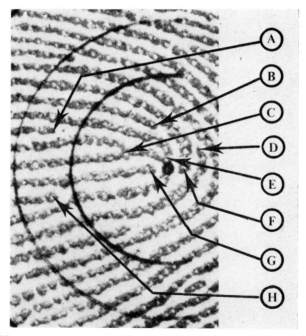

Figure 99A. Figure 99 enlarged. Seven ridge characteristics are disclosed within specified perimeters. (A), ridge end characteristic; (B), ridge end characteristic; (C), bifurcation characteristic; (D), partial recurving ridge extending beyond loop apex and is *perimeter "A." Exclude* as a ridge characteristic. (E), bifurcation characteristic, forming part and attached to the first recurving ridge; (F), partial recurving ridge does *not* extend beyond loop apex but is enclosed by characteristic "D." *Include as a ridge end characteristic.* (G), ridge end characteristic; (H), ridge end characteristic.

TABLE II

ANALYSIS OF SECONDARY SUBCLASSIFICATION LOOP CORE RIGHT HAND

Number of Ridge Characteristics in Core	"I" Loop %	"O" Loop %	"D" Loop %	"U" Loop %	"K" Loop %	Total %
O (zero)	3.6	1.6	1.0	.2	—	6.4
1	.4	1.0	—	.4	—	1.8
2	.8	3.6	.6	.4	.2	5.6
3	3.0	6.0	.8	.8	—	10.6
4	2.8	8.2	.6	.6	.2	12.4
5	3.0	7.4	1.2	.6	.2	12.4
6	2.8	7.4	.8	.6	.6	12.2
7	2.6	7.0	.8	1.0	.6	12.0
8	1.8	3.0	.6	.2	.2	5.8
9	1.4	3.0	.4	.8	.2	5.8
10	.8	3.2	1.0	.2	.2	5.4
11	1.6	.8	.4	—	.2	3.0
12	.4	1.2	.6	—	.2	2.4
13	.8	.4	.4	—	—	1.6
14	.2	.4	.4	.2	—	1.2
15+	.4	.8	—	—	.2	1.4
Total	26.4	55.0	9.6	6.0	3.0	100

Analysis of variation of ridge characteristics in 1,000 *random* loop cores of the *right hand*. Summary shows probable search ratio for each of the 5 loop patterns with any given loop core. Alternative search ratio can be estimated when search is confined to 2 ridge characteristics either side of given number. This table should be read in conjunction with Table VI when allocating filing schedules.

TABLE III

ANALYSIS OF SECONDARY SUBCLASSIFICATION LOOP CORE LEFT HAND

Number of Ridge Characteristics in Core	"I" Loop %	"O" Loop %	"D" Loop %	"U" Loop %	"K" Loop %	Total %
O (zero)	4.4	4.0	.8	.2	.2	9.6
1	.8	2.4	.2	—	—	3.4
2	1.6	3.6	.4	.2	.2	6.0
3	1.8	7.0	.8	.4	—	10.0
4	5.0	7.0	—	.2	—	12.2
5	4.8	8.0	.2	—	.2	13.2
6	3.6	6.4	.8	.2	.2	11.2
7	3.6	6.0	.2	—	—	9.8
8	1.8	3.4	.4	.2	.2	6.0
9	1.8	4.0	.2	—	—	6.0
10	1.0	1.8	.2	.2	—	3.2
11	1.8	1.0	—	—	.2	3.0
12	.8	.6	—	—	.2	1.6
13	.4	.8	—	—	—	1.2
14	.4	.8	.4	.2	—	1.8
15+	1.0	.2	.4	.2	—	1.8
Total	34.6	57.0	5.0	2.0	1.4	100

Analysis of variation of ridge characteristics in 1,000 *random* loop cores of the *left hand*. Summary shows probables search ratio for each of the 5 loop patterns with any given loop core. Alternative search ratio can be estimated when search is confined to 2 ridge characteristics either side of given number. This table should be read in conjunction with Table VII when allocating filing schedules.

DELTA TYPES

Subclassification of High "H" and Low "L" Deltas in the Hypothenar Section

The subclassification is *only* used when the hypothenar section is devoid of pattern(s).

The carpal delta is situated in the hypothenar section of the palm and is formed by three ridge streams converging, thus producing a deltaic or triradiate formation (Figs. 1, 93, and 94).

For the purposes of the subclassification the innermost ridges of the three ridge streams form the perimeter ridges. These ridges can do the following:

1. Converge at a point thus:

2. Join one another forming converging points thus:

3. Run side by side thus:

4. Assume composite forms of items 2 and 3 thus:

In items 2, 3, and 4, the perimeter ridges create a space which is bounded by the converging points and/or where two ridges running side by side diverge. The delta area cannot be precisely defined, but the perimeter ridges must continue past the points of convergence and/or place where the divergence begins (Fig. 100). The occurrence or nonoccurrence of characteristics within the perimeter ridges form seven delta types "A" to "G" and are recorded in square "C" of the coding box. (See Figs. 101 to 107 and line drawings of delta types in Diagram II.)

Disregard any characteristic(s) *attached* to or *forming part* of the three perimeter ridges (Fig. 100).

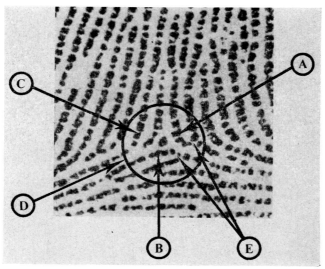

Figure 100. (A), perimeter ridge; (B), perimeter ridge; (C), perimeter ridge; (D), approximate delta area; (E), indicates two ridge characteristics attached to and forming part of perimeter ridges "A" and "B."

Delta Types

Delta Type "A"

The three ridges comprising the perimeter *converge* and there are *no* characteristics within the perimeter (Fig. 101).

Delta Type "B"

Where at least one of the three ridges forming the perimeter runs side by side with another and within the perimeter there are *no* characteristics (Fig. 102) except where there is *one* ridge intervening that stops abruptly. The ridge end is in fact the delta.

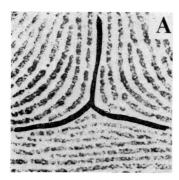

Figure 101. Darkened ridges indicate perimeter ridges.

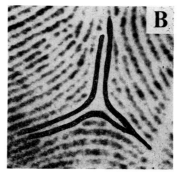

Figure 102. Darkened ridges indicate perimeter ridges.

Delta Type "C"

Where any or all of the three ridges forming the perimeter either converge or run side by side and within the perimeter there is present a *single dot* (Fig. 103) or, a *single small independent* ridge.

Delta Type "D"

Where any or all of the three ridges forming the perimeter either converge or run side by side and within the perimeter is present any *dot with* any combination of dot(s), independent ridge(s), or ridge(s) ending abruptly (Fig. 104).

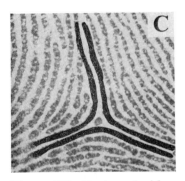

Figure 103. Darkened ridges indicate perimeter ridges.

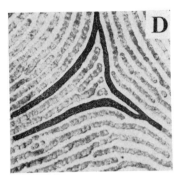

Figure 104. Darkened ridges indicate perimeter ridges.

Delta Type "E"

Where any or all of the three ridges forming the perimeter either converge or run side by side and within the perimeter there is present any combination of independent ridge(s) and/or ridge(s) ending abruptly (Fig. 105) *excluding any dot(s).*

Delta Type "F"

Where any or all of the three ridges forming the perimeter either converge or run side by side and within the perimeter there is present an unattached lake, or an unattached ridge bearing a spur, lake, or bifurcation (Fig. 106). *All other characteristics are disregarded.*

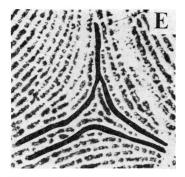

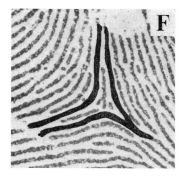

Figure 105. Darkened ridges indicate perimeter ridges.

Figure 106. Darkened ridges indicate perimeter ridges.

Delta Type "G"

Where a flexure crease or scar renders classification impossible (Fig. 107).

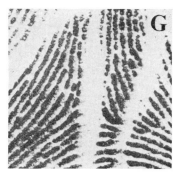

Figure 107. Delta obliterated by perpendicular flexion crease.

Record as "H" in square "C" of the coding box, when it is not possible to code the delta because of the following:
1. Delta is not disclosed.
2. A badly taken palmprint form.
3. Delta has been omitted from palmprint form.

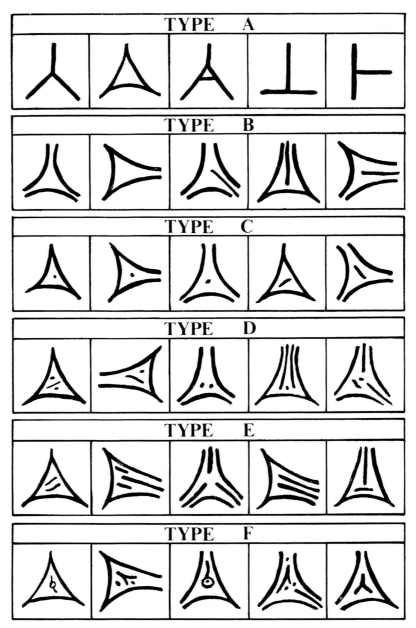

Diagram II. Examples of delta types. It is to be assumed that each of the perimeter ridges depicted extends beyond the delta area.

TABLE IV

ANALYSIS OF SECONDARY SUBCLASSIFICATION (DELTAS) RIGHT HAND

Delta Type	High "H"	Low "L"	Total
	%	%	%
A	6.4	14.9	21.3
B	2.2	4.5	6.7
C	4.2	13.2	17.4
D	8.3	17.0	25.3
E	7.8	14.0	21.8
F	.9	1.9	2.8
G	.5	3.2	3.7
H	.2	.8	1.0
Total	30.5	69.5	100

Analysis of delta types in 1,000 *random right hand* forms. Summary shows probable search ratio for any given delta type with high or low delta. This table should be read in conjunction with Table VI when allocating filing schedules.

TABLE V

ANALYSIS OF SECONDARY SUBCLASSIFICATION (DELTAS) LEFT HAND

Delta Type	High "H"	Low "L"	Total
	%	%	%
A	5.6	15.2	20.8
B	1.3	4.7	6.0
C	6.0	15.4	21.4
D	7.9	18.1	26.0
E	6.5	13.1	19.6
F	.6	1.8	2.4
G	.6	2.1	2.7
H	.3	.8	1.1
Total	28.8	71.2	100

Analysis of delta types in 1,000 *random left hand* forms. Summary shows probable search ratio for any given delta type with high or low delta. This table should be read in conjunction with Table VII when allocating filing schedules.

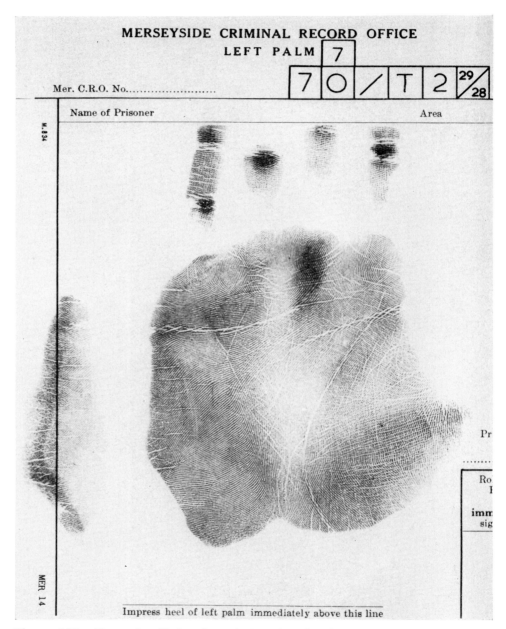

Figure 108.   Example of left palmar impression showing completed classification.

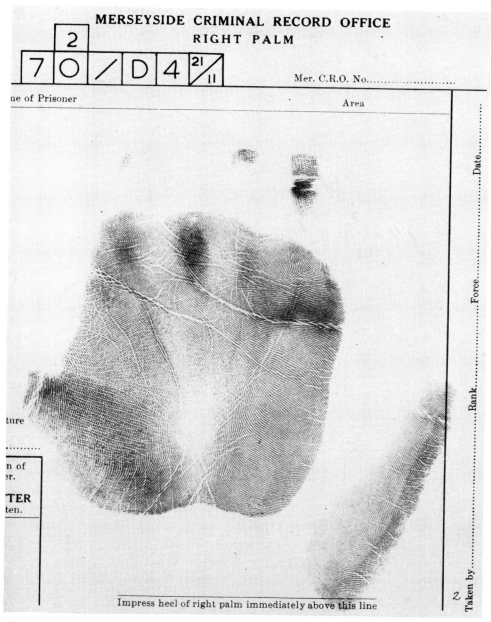

Figure 109. Example of right palmar impression showing completed classification.

Chapter X

FILING SEQUENCES

To assist in the association of certain of the sectional classifications with the appropriate squares in the coding box, reference is made by a letter to that square, i.e. primary—square "A" coding box.

Primary Classification

(All three sections—square "A" coding box.)

Order

1–2–3–4–5–6–7–9

Secondary Classification

(Hypothenar section—square "B" coding box.)

Order

A–B–TL–LP–CP–ACC–T–I–O–D–U–K–N–H–L

Whorl   Loop   Delta

Where two patterns are disclosed in one section the form is filed *after* the single pattern of whichever symbol is shown on top, i.e. if symbol "A" is on the top, symbol "I" beneath, the form is filed after the single "A" symbol in the sequence as above, viz. A/A–A/B–A/TL–A/LP–A/CP–A/ACC–A/T–A/I, and so forth. If the symbol "B" is on top and symbol "I" beneath, the form is filed after the single "B" symbol in the following sequence B/A–B/B–B/TL–B/LP–B/CP–B/ACC–B/T–B/I, and so forth.

Where three patterns are disclosed in one section the form is filed after the double pattern in progressive sequence, i.e. double pattern A/A–triple pattern A/A/A–A/A/B–A/A/TL to A/A/N, double pattern CP/I–triple pattern CP/I/A–CP/I/B–CP/I/TL to CP/I/N.

Secondary Subclassification

(Hypothenar section—square "C" coding box. Recorded when any of the following is present in the hypothenar section: "H" or "L" delta, or, single loop of the type "I," "O," "D," "U," or "K.")

94

Order

Filed in progression *after* the appropriate secondary classification and *before* the tertiary and/or quaternary classification (when present). Exhausting the tertiary and/or quaternary classification *before* commencing the next subclassification. Thereby arriving at a complete tertiary and/or quaternary classification *between* each subclassification.

Tertiary Classification

(Thenar section—square "D" coding box.)

Order

Same as for secondary classification.

Quaternary Classification

Order: Parts 1 and 2

(Triradiate section—squares "E" and "F" coding box.)

Part 1 is the same as for secondary classification.

Part 2 is filed in numerical order *after* each symbol, i.e. A.2—A.4, and so on; double patterns D/D 4—D/D 6, and so on.

Order: Part 3

(Triradiate section—square "G" coding box.)

The ridge counts on the bottom are filed first; when the top number is

TABLE VI
(See next page.)

Table VI is an analysis of a complete *right hand* collection of 5,976 forms, showing the following:
1. The disposition of pattern(s) over the entire palmar surface.
2. The probable search ratio in any *one* or *more* palmar sections, whether patternless, *or,* with any pattern, *or,* combination of patterns.
3. The number of forms with the same or similar main line of configuration, which can be ascertained by adding or subtracting certain of the primary and secondary codings with the key headings and vice-versa.
4. The space required when allocating filing schedules. This table should be read in conjunction with Tables II and IV.
Not included in the table are the following:
1. Ridge count variations in the triradiate section.
2. Secondary subclassification variations, loop and delta types.
3. Number of forms in each of the ten-year age cycle.

Note: Forms comprising collection *only* include the palmprints of persons charged with offences of robbery; burglary and like offences; theft of, and from, motor vehicles; some cases of murder and manslaughter, and any other offence where the person charged is likely to have left a latent print at the scene.

TABLE VI

ANALYSIS OF RIGHT HAND COLLECTION

Primary and Secondary Coding	Triradiate (a)	(b)	Ridge Count (c)	(d)	(e)	(f)	(g)	(h)	(j)	(k)	(l)	(m)	(n)
1 H	48								48	.8			
1 L	111								111	1.8			
2 H	2								2	.03			
2 L	2								2	.03			
3 H		4	75	22	173	375	114	36	799	13.3	799	649	114
3 L		2	265	77	831	1019	302	57	2553	42.6	2553	2194	302
4 (A-B-TL-LP (CP-ACC-T	19								19	.31			
4 I	29								29	.47			
4 O	48								48	.8			
4 D-U-K-N	26								26	.43			
5 H			1		4	19	12	1	37	.62	37	24	12
5 L			15	2	50	63	40	14	184	3.06	184	130	40
6 (A-B-TL-LP (CP-ACC-T													
6 I	2								2	.03			
6 O	1								1	.01			
6 D-U-K-N													
7 (A-B-LP (ACC-T			14	4	34	47	17	4	120	2.0	120	99	17
7 TL			13	6	32	53	25	2	131	2.18	131	104	25
7 CP		2	9	2	18	25	8	1	65	1.08	65	56	8
7 I		7	31	12	82	171	61	12	376	6.14	376	303	61
7 O		3	92	25	250	383	113	19	885	14.7	885	753	113
7 O/I			5		14	26	7	4	56	.9	56	45	7
7 D		1	25	4	75	73	22	6	206	3.4	206	178	22
7 U-K-N		3	20	13	46	83	21	6	192	3.2	192	165	21
9 (A-B-TL-LP (CP-ACC-T			2		2	3	2	1	10	.16	10	7	2
9 I			2		3	14	5	2	26	.43	26	19	5
9 O			2	1	9	13	6	7	38	.62	38	25	6
9 D-U-K-N			2		2	3	1	2	10	.16	10	7	1
Total	288	22	573	168	1625	2370	756	174	5976		5688	4758	756
Approx. % of collection	4.8	.36	9.6	2.8	27.1	39.4	12.6	2.9		95.0	79.2	12.6	

(a) Number of forms *without* pattern in triradiate.

(b) Number of forms *with* single pattern of either A-B-TL-LP-CP-ACC in triradiate.

(c) Number of forms *with* "T" in triradiate.

(d) Number of forms *with* "I" in triradiate.

(e) Number of forms *with* "D2" in triradiate.

(f) Number of forms *with* "D4" in triradiate.

(g) Number of forms *with* double pattern in triradiate.

(h) Number of forms *with* 3 or more patterns in triradiate.

(j) Total number of forms in collection under review the figure of 6,000 is used for assessing various percentages.

(k) Approximate % of collection.

(l) Number of forms *with* pattern in triradiate.

(m) Number of forms *with* single pattern in triradiate.

(n) Number of forms *with* double pattern in triradiate.

(o) Number of forms *with* 3 or more patterns in triradiate.

(p) Number of forms *without* pattern in hypothenar.

(p)	(q)	(r)	(s)	(t)	(u)	(v)	(w)	(x)	(y)	(z)	(aa)	(ab)	(ac)
48		48	48										
111		111		111									
2			2		2	2							
2				2	2	2							
799		799	799										
2553		2553		2553									
	19	19											
	29	29											
	48	48											
	26	26											
37			37		37		24	12	1				
184				184	184		130	40	14				
					0	0							
	2				2	2							
	1				1	1							
					0	0							
	120	120								120	99	17	4
	131	131								131	104	25	2
	65	65								65	56	8	1
	376	376								376	303	61	12
	885	885								885	753	113	19
	56	56								56	45	7	4
	206	206								206	178	22	6
	192	192								192	165	21	6
	10				10		7	2	1				
	26				26		19	5	2				
	38				38		25	6	7				
	10				10		7	1	2				
3736	2240	5664	886	2850	312	7	212	66	27	2031	1703	274	54
62.5	37.5	94.8	14.8	47.7	5.2	.116	3.5	1.1	.45	33.8	28.4	4.57	.90

(q) Number of forms *with* pattern in hypothenar.

(r) Number of forms *without* pattern in thenar.

(s) Number of forms *with* "H" delta in hypothenar.

(t) Number of forms *with* "L" delta in hypothenar.

(u) Number of forms *with* pattern in thenar.

(v) Number of forms *with* pattern in thenar and *no* pattern in triradiate.

(w) Number of forms *with* pattern in thenar and *single* pattern in triradiate.

(x) Number of forms *with* pattern in thenar and *double* pattern in triradiate.

(y) Number of forms with pattern in thenar and *3 or more* patterns in triradiate.

(z) Number of forms *with* pattern(s) in hypothenar and triradiate.

(aa) Number of forms *with* pattern(s) in hypothenar and *single* pattern in triradiate.

(ab) Number of forms *with* pattern(s) in hypothenar and *double* pattern in triradiate.

(ac) Number of forms *with* pattern(s) in hypothenar and *3 or more* patterns in triradiate.

exhausted the next number on the bottom is then filed, i.e. 1/1—2/1—3/1—4/1—5/1, and so forth, then 1/2—2/2—3/2—4/2—5/2, and so forth, then 1/3—2/3—3/3—4/3—5/3, and so forth.

If no pattern, symbol, or numeric value is disclosed, a diagonal line is drawn across the appropriate square of the coding box. This will ensure that no single factor of the classification is omitted in error.

Care must be taken to ensure that the full classification is recorded on the nominal index slip. The right hand classification is recorded above that of the left hand (Fig. 110).

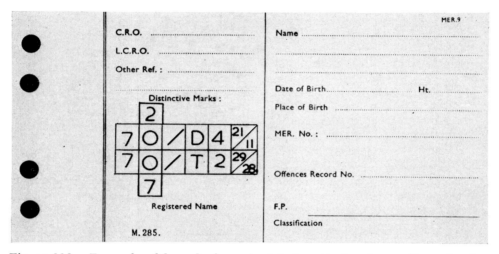

Figure 110.   Example of loose-leaf nominal index slip bearing coding of palmprints in Figures 108 and 109.

Palmprint forms recording both left and right palmar impressions should be cut in two, each hand to be filed separately, thus creating a two-hand palmar filing system. Separate collections based on the geographical structure served by the bureau is advised, with a further breakdown of a ten-year age cycle within each of the collections.

Similarly, palmprints found at a scene of crime are classified as far as possible and filed in area and pattern order in accordance with the system. A duplicate photograph for each palmprint is also filed in numerical order in a separate collection which is divided into geographical areas.

TABLE VII

(See next page.)

Table VII is an analysis of a complete *left hand* collection of 6,076 forms, showing the following:

1. The disposition of pattern(s) over the entire palmar surface.

2. The probable search ratio in any *one* or *more* palmar sections, whether patternless, *or,* with any pattern, *or,* combination of patterns.

3. The number of forms with the same or similar main line of configuration, which can be ascertained by adding or subtracting certain of the primary and secondary codings with the key headings and vice-versa.

4. The space required when allocating filing schedules. This table should be read in conjunction with Tables III and V.

Not included in the table are the following:

1. Ridge count variations in the triradiate section.

2. Secondary subclassification variations, loop and delta types.

3. Number of forms in each of the ten-year age cycle.

Note: Forms comprising collection *only* include the palmprints of persons charged with offences of robbery; burglary and like offences; theft of, and from, motor vehicles; some cases of murder and manslaughter, and any other offence where the person charged is likely to have left a latent print at the scene.

TABLE VII

ANALYSIS OF LEFT HAND COLLECTION

Primary and Secondary Coding	(a)	(b)	Triradiate — Ridge Count (c)	(d)	(e)	(f)	(g)	(h)	(j)	(k)	(l)	(m)	(n)
1 H	79								79	1.3			
1 L	158								158	2.6			
2 H	6								6	.09			
2 L	14								14	.23			
3 H		8	117	117	166	131	142	16	697	11.5	697	539	142
3 L		20	428	406	1035	410	347	24	2670	44.0	2670	2299	347
4 (A-B-TL-LP (CP-ACC-T	9								9	.14			
4 I	17								17	.28			
4 O	65								65	1.07			
4 D-U-K-N	13								13	.21			
5 H		1	9	12	21	23	30	5	101	1.66	101	66	30
5 L		9	50	35	109	71	74	14	362	5.95	362	274	74
6 (A-B-TL-LP (CP-ACC-T									—				
6 I	2								2	.03			
6 O	7								7	.11			
6 D-U-K-N									—				
7 (A-B-LP (ACC-T		1	8	9	13	5	3	—	39	.64	39	36	3
7 TL			15	10	20	17	17	—	79	1.3	79	62	17
7 CP			4	3	12	7	5	1	32	.53	32	26	5
7 I		4	80	62	131	88	50	1	416	6.8	416	365	50
7 O		5	151	128	272	136	147	8	847	13.9	847	692	147
7 O/I			13	13	28	18	16	5	93	1.52	93	72	16
7 D		1	21	14	47	13	17	3	116	1.9	116	96	17
7 U-K-N			7	13	8	13	13	1	55	.9	55	41	13
9 (A-B-TL-LP (CP-ACC-T			2	2	3	3	1	4	15	.24	15	10	1
9 I		2	5	1	17	6	10	5	46	.75	46	31	10
9 O		1	13	14	31	22	38	4	123	2.25	123	81	38
9 D-U-K-N			1	1	4	3	5	1	15	.24	15	9	5
Total	370	52	924	840	1917	966	915	92	6076		5706	4699	915
Approx. % of collection	6.08	.858	15.2	13.8	31.6	15.9	15.1	1.52			94.0	77.2	15.1

(a) Number of forms *without* pattern in triradiate.

(b) Number of forms *with* single pattern of either A-B-TL-LP-CP-ACC in triradiate.

(c) Number of forms *with* "T" in triradiate.

(d) Number of forms *with* "I" in triradiate.

(e) Number of forms *with* "D2" in triradiate.

(f) Number of forms *with* "D4" in triradiate.

(g) Number of forms *with* double pattern in triradiate.

(h) Number of forms *with* 3 or more patterns in triradiate.

(j) Total number of forms in collection under review the figure of 6,075 is used for assessing various percentages.

(k) Approximate % of collection.

(l) Number of forms *with* pattern in triradiate.

(m) Number of forms *with* single pattern in triradiate.

(n) Number of forms *with* double pattern in triradiate.

(o) Number of forms *with* 3 or more patterns in triradiate.

(p) Number of forms *without* pattern in hypothenar.

(p)	(q)	(r)	(s)	(t)	(u)	(v)	(w)	(x)	(y)	(z)	(aa)	(ab)	(ac)
79		79	79										
158		158		158									
6			6		6	6							
14				14	14	14							
697		697	697										
2670		2670		2670									
	9	9											
	17	17											
	65	65											
	13	13											
101			101		101		66	30	5				
362				362	362		274	74	14				
	2				2	2							
	7				7	7							
	39	39								39	36	3	—
	79	79								79	62	17	—
	32	32								32	26	5	1
	416	416								416	365	50	1
	847	847								847	692	147	8
	93	93								93	72	16	5
	116	116								116	96	17	3
	55	55								55	41	13	1
	15				15		10	1	4				
	46				46		31	10	5				
	123				123		81	38	4				
	15				15		9	5	1				
4087	1989	5385	883	3204	691	29	471	158	33	1677	1390	268	19
67.4	32.6	88.8	14.6	52.8	11.2	.477	7.7	2.6	.54	27.7	22.9	4.4	.031

(q) Number of forms *with* pattern in hypothenar.

(r) Number of forms *without* pattern in thenar.

(s) Number of forms *with* "H" delta in hypothenar.

(t) Number of forms *with* "L" delta in hypothenar.

(u) Number of forms *with* pattern in thenar.

(v) Number of forms *with* patterns in thenar and *no* pattern in triradiate.

(w) Number of forms *with* pattern in thenar and *single* pattern in triradiate.

(x) Number of forms *with* pattern in thenar and *double* pattern in triradiate.

(y) Number of forms with pattern in thenar and *3 or more* patterns in triradiate.

(z) Number of forms *with* pattern(s) in hypothenar and triradiate.

(aa) Number of forms *with* pattern(s) in hypothenar and *single* pattern in triradiate.

(ab) Number of forms *with* pattern(s) in hypothenar and *double* pattern in triradiate.

(ac) Number of forms *with* pattern(s) in hypothenar and *3 or more* patterns in triradiate.

Chapter XI

PAPILLARY RIDGES
STRUCTURE – CHARACTERISTICS – PERSISTANCE

The skin covering the surface of the palms, the soles of the feet, the fingers and toes, differs markedly from the rest of the body surface. It is entirely without hair which, even minutely, covers the rest of the body. It is without pigment or coloring matter which, even in a white person, is present elsewhere in some quantity. It is covered entirely with minute ridges, commonly referred to as friction or papillary ridges. The ridges exist because many layers of skin and tissue form themselves over the body of the sweat glands. The ducts of the sweat glands exit along the crests of the ridges and due to their close proximity, the sweat forms an almost continuous flow along the top of the ridges which, when impressed, leaves a latent imprint.

These ridges have been described in many ways from a resemblance to ridges made on sand by wind and flowing water to the appearance of corduroy cloth. Each ridge is characterized by numerous minute peculiarities called papillary minutiae which may assume any of the following characteristics:

1. The ridge bifurcates.
2. The ridge bifurcates and unites with another.
3. The ridge terminates abruptly.
4. The ridge encloses a circular or elliptical space.
5. The ridge possesses a spur or a hook.
6. The ridge is so short as to be independent.
7. The ridge is so short as to form a dot or an island.

The ridges are said to be first discernible in the fourth month of fetal life and fully formed by the sixth. They grow simultaneously with the general growth of the body. They persist and remain constant throughout life unless their symmetry is permanently disturbed by a deep-seated injury.

Evidence about palmprints is now accepted by the courts in the same way as evidence about fingerprints. In respect of footprints, very few cases have been *proved* and this is why some courts are hesitant to accept the validity and the opinion of the fingerprint expert. In all cases, the expert must carefully prepare his testimony and be able to explain in detail to the satisfaction of both judge and jury the fact that papillary detail is not confined merely to the fingers and palms.

Anatomically, there is no difference between footprints, palmprints, or fingerprints as far as identification is concerned. The ridges on the plantar and palmar surfaces have all the attributes, physical characteristics, and identification requisites as do those on the ends of the fingers. The treatment of a footprint or palmprint so far as its preparation for court, mode of proof, comparison, and identification is exactly the same as for fingerprint evidence.

The accuracy of any such identification, whether by foot, toe, palm, or finger is based on the following facts: that the characteristics of the ridges are formed on the palmar and plantar skin of the body before birth and remain constant until decomposition after death; that no two separate individuals have exactly the same arrangement of the details disclosed in their papillary ridges; that in practical experience throughout the world no two fingerprints, palmprints, or soleprints have been found which are identical in the sequence of their ridge characteristics, and that conservative mathematical calculations indicate the extreme improbability of a chance duplication.

Chapter XII

TAKING PALMPRINTS

Correctly taken palmprints are of paramount importance as only those of a high standard should be included in the collections. The ultimate result should be a clearly defined impression of the whole palm embracing the three main sections, taken with the minimum of ridge distortion and without smudging or double impressions.

To achieve this, several factors must be borne in mind.

1. The correct equipment should be used.

2. The equipment should be kept clean, and after use all traces of ink should be removed.

3. The hands of the subject should have been recently washed with soap and water and thoroughly dried—eliminating excess perspiration and foreign matter from the furrows and promoting fresh perspiration along the ridges.

4. Complete control of the hand when in contact with the paper. Experience will show the required amount of pressure which should be applied. Too little will result in an incomplete impression, too much will cause distortion.

EQUIPMENT REQUIRED

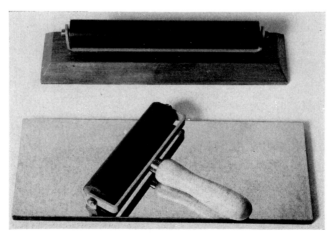

Figure 111. Palmprint-taking equipment: palm roller; ink plate and ink roller.

Ink Plate

A polished metal plate mounted on a wooden block or a piece of 1/4-inch plate glass with bevelled edges measuring 12 inches by 5 inches on which to spread the ink.

Ink Roller

A resilient rubber or composition roller 5 inches wide for distributing the ink on both the inking plate and the surface of the palm. The roller should be maintained in such a manner as to allow it to revolve easily.

Palm Roller

An 8-inch resilient rubber or composition roller supported at either end to allow it to revolve freely.

Inking the Plate

Four or five drops of fingerprint ink evenly dispersed over the surface of the plate by the ink roller is usually sufficient to provide the required consistency. Additional ink may be required if the skin is dry. After rolling, the ink should have the appearance of a matt finish; too much, and the ink will appear too black and shiny. A test can be made by taking a trial finger impression. Any surplus ink can be removed by placing a piece of paper over the plate and rolling, repeating the process until the correct amount of ink remains.

Inking the Palm

The ink roller only should be used for inking the palm. Use only a light pressure—if the pressure is too great, the ink will be forced into the furrows. The ink should be evenly dispersed over the whole palmar area, paying special attention to the extreme top edge of the triradiate section including the third joint of the fingers and the metacarpo phalangeal creases, and also the extreme base including part of the wrist and carpal flexion crease.

METHODS OF TAKING PALMPRINTS

The Plain Impression

Ensure that the thumb and fingers are in line with the palm, place the inked palm on the paper, pressing gently on the back of the hand (Fig. 112). Some operators think that this is an ideal method of taking palmprints. However, in my experience serious faults emerge, in that the centre and extreme top edge of the triradiate section and the base of the palm near the carpal delta may *not* be recorded. In addition, extreme distortion is likely to occur.

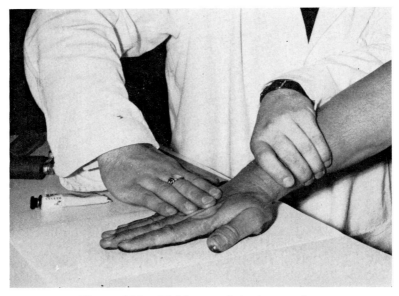

Figure 112.   Taking a plain impression.

Rolled Impression — Using the Palm Roller

ROLLING PALM FROM WRIST TO FINGERS. Place wrist of subject on the paper (Fig. 113), apply gentle pressure on the back of the hand, roll inked palm across the roller to the fingers. The palm should be slowly rolled

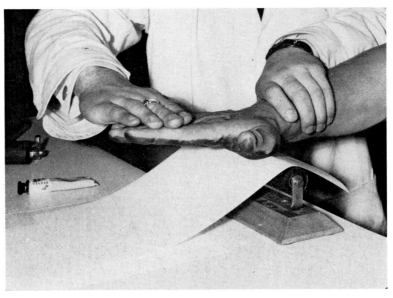

Figure 113.   Taking a rolled impression, wrist to finger method.

across the paper; if not, distortion of the ridges in the thenar and carpal delta areas may occur.

ROLLING PALM FROM FINGERS TO WRIST. Use the same method as above but place the fingers on paper (see Fig. 114) and roll to wrist, including the carpal flexion crease. This is by far the most satisfactory method of taking palmprints because less distortion occurs and a complete palmar impression is more easily obtained.

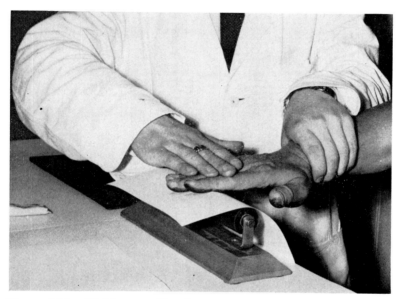

Figure 114. Taking a rolled impression, finger to wrist method.

Rolled Impression of Outside of Hypothenar

In addition, a rolled impression of the outside of the hypothenar section should be taken. The outer edge of the hypothenar section should be re-inked and placed on the paper in the manner shown in Figure 115, rolling the palm inward.

Figure 115.   Taking a rolled impression of the outside edge of the hypothenar section.

This additional information has a twofold advantage in that

1. There are occasions when a plain or rolled impression is obtained, that certain characteristics, such as a recurving ridge, a pattern, or a delta which is present in the outside edge of this section is not recorded. If this fact is not observed at the time and the additional rolled impression is not taken, it is possible that an incorrect classification will ensue.

2. As this area of the palm is most frequently found at a scene of crime, any detail omitted from the palmprint form will make any identification all the more difficult to compare.

Chapter XIII

SEARCHING THE CLASSIFIED COLLECTION

Searching a latent palmprint discovered at a scene of crime with the classified collection is not as difficult as it first appears. Knowledge of ridge
construction of the palmar surface is an asset but is not essential, providing
the operator has the ability to identify papillary minutiae.

Before commencing a search, three factors should be borne in mind in
order to minimize the risk of an abortive or time-consuming search.

First, all scene-of-crime marks should have been fully eliminated with
those persons having legitimate access to the venue in which the mark was
discovered.

Second, whether or not the mark is capable of search. Without doubt,
all marks bearing sufficient ridge detail are capable of search, providing
that time and manpower are available. Usually, a search is confined to
those marks which bear either a pattern, delta, or discernible flexion
crease or where there is a reasonable chance of success during a limited time.

Third, whether or not it is possible to ascertain the section and hand
from which the mark emanates. In some cases it is more difficult to establish
the hand than the section.

A palmar impression from any of the three sections, whether partial or
complete, is capable of search. It is a simple matter to arrive at the appropriate part of the collection by merely eliminating certain of the primary,
secondary, tertiary, or quaternary classifications.

The average palmprint contains some 14 square inches of ridge detail
on its surface. When considered, this is an extremely large area of scrutiny,
especially when most impressions submitted are fragments.

It is worthy of note that each section of the palm bears its own main
line of configuration. The presence of a pattern will disturb the flow of
ridges and create a different configuration, which is common to that pattern.

The presence of such patterns, deltas, flexion creases, and the configuration of ridges, will to some degree assist in determining section and in
differentiating between one hand and another.

It is not always possible to lay down hard-and-fast rules regarding the
mode of search or the establishment of the hand or section from which a
scene-of-crime mark emanates. However, the following observations will
assist.

TRIRADIATE SECTION

This section is easily the most recognizable because of the ridge configuration and the presence of numerous deltas. In addition, of all palmprints recorded, about 95 percent contain one or more patterns in this section.

The distal transverse crease is a most useful feature when defining the correct hand for search purposes. It travels horizontally beneath the little, ring, and middle fingers and suddenly slopes to and exits between the middle and forefingers. The outer edge of the crease beneath the little finger comprises a number of minute creases converging into the main stream at an angle.

The inner loop "I" formation originates between the little and ring fingers making a definite slope beneath the ring finger and points markedly toward the extreme top edge of the thenar section. As only a few outer loop "O" formations are disclosed in this section, it is almost safe to assume that the pattern is an inner loop "I" on the opposite hand.

The arch and tented arch formations are usually disclosed beneath the ring finger, even when the pattern constitutes part of a multipattern sequence.

In most cases, the overall ridge counts of the downward loop "D" formation will act as a guide to its position in the section. The smaller the numeric value, the larger the overall ridge count. Those loops in the 8 position are smaller in ridge counts than those in the 4 position; conversely, those in the 2 position usually have the larger count.

THENAR

This section is completely enclosed by the radial longitudinal crease.

In about 95 percent of all palmprints recorded, the section is patternless and the ridge structure resembles that of a large arch formation.

In the remaining 5 percent of forms, patterns are disclosed. They are usually very distinctive in appearance and unusual in composition. It therefore follows that when a scene-of-crime mark bearing a pattern in the thenar section (whether or not other sections are disclosed) is submitted, the search is both short and speedy.

Minor creases traverse the section in various directions and often help to establish the area of ridge scrutiny.

Because of the ridge structure, it is ofen a simple matter to define both the section and hand from which the latent print emanates.

HYPOTHENAR

To assist in defining the correct hand, the ridge structure, the presence of a pattern, or a delta will often act as a guide. A special note should be made of those ridges which converge at the top centre of the section; compare with the ridge formation in a similar position in Figure 2.

When an inner "I" loop formation is present, it is accompanied by two deltas, one forming itself above the loop recurve, the other beneath, usually at the base of the palm in the carpal area. The deltas and recurve are disposed on the inside of the palm in close proximity to the thenar section, giving a good indication as to hand.

Whereas in the outer "O" loop formation, the ridges form and slope away from the delta in the carpal area toward a delta on the outside edge of the section. Rarely is this latter delta disclosed unless (1) it is in close proximity to the loop recurve, or (2) the outside edge of the palm has been recorded on the palmprint form in the prescribed manner.

Minute creases often appear on the outside edge of this section beneath the little finger, the majority of which run horizontally.

The radial longitudinal crease, more often than not, bifurcates near the carpal delta and travels to some degree into the hypothenar section.

TABLE VIII

SUMMARY OF IDENTIFICATIONS FROM SEPTEMBER 1964 TO DECEMBER 1969

Pattern Types		1964/5	1966	1967	1968	1969	Total
Hypothenar	A	1	—	—	—	—	1
	B	—	1	—	1	—	2
	T.L.	2	—	3	3	2	10
	L.P.	—	—	—	—	—	—
	C.P.	2	—	1	1	2	6
	A.C.C.	1	—	—	—	1	2
	T	1	—	—	—	3	4
	I	7	6	8	4	6	31
	O	13	6	13	9	11	52
	O/I	2	1	1	1	1	6
	D	2	4	—	2	1	9
	U	1	3	3	—	1	8
	K	1	—	1	—	—	2
	N	—	1	—	2	2	5
	H delta	1	1	5	3	2	12
	L delta	—	4	5	—	3	12
	Indefinite	1	1	—	9	7	18
	Right hand	19	17*	22*	20*	24*	102*
	Left hand	16	11*	18*	15*	18*	78*
Triradiate	Single pattern	2	3	1	6	5	17
	Two or more patterns	—	1	1	—	3	5
	Indefinite	—	1	1	—	1	3
	Right hand	2	2*	1*	2*	5*	12*
	Left hand	—	3*	2*	4*	4*	13*
Thenar	Pattern(s)	1	2	1	1	5	10
	Indefinite	—	—	2	2	3	7
	Right hand	—	—	2*	2*	5*	9*
	Left hand	1	2*	1*	1*	3*	8*

TABLE VIII *(cont.)*

		1964/5	1966	1967	1968	1969	Total
(a)	Persons *not* in custody and not suspected.	19	11	13	14	27	84
(b)	Persons in custody and not suspected.	19	15	16	15	22	87
(c)	Persons suspected. Identifications include only those cases where, by request, a named suspect was compared. The request was with a number of offences where latent prints were discovered and *not* just one specified offence.	—	7	16	13	7	43
	Total	38	33	45	42	56	214
(d)	Cases where a palmprint only was found at scene of crime.	21	24	25	23	30	123
(e)	Cases where finger and palmprints were found at the scene of crime and palmprint *only* was identical.	17	5	14	12	16	64
(f)	Cases where finger and palmprints were found at the scene of crime and both were identical but the palmprint was initial identification.	—	4	6	7	10	27
	Total	38	33	45	42	56	214

*Included in the summary and certain of the totals are those cases where more than one section of the palm was discovered at the scene of crime. Both sections were identified as the same person.

INDEX